INVENTORY 1985

Hitler Youth
and
Catholic Youth

HITLER YOUTH
AND
CATHOLIC YOUTH 1933-1936

A Study in Totalitarian Conquest

by

Lawrence D. Walker
Illinois State University

THE CATHOLIC UNIVERSITY OF AMERICA PRESS
Washington, D.C. 20017

Library of Congress Catalog No. 75 - 114984
SBN - 8132 - 0499 - 2

to My Parents

TABLE OF CONTENTS

Acknowledgments

To thank those who have been of assistance in the research and writing of this book is to review a treasured portion of my life. I wish to thank especially Professor Raymond J. Sontag of the University of California, Berkeley, who read the manuscript in its original form, as did Professors Gerald Feldman and Paul Seabury, also of Berkeley. I wish to thank the Committee on Research of the University of California, Berkeley, for providing me with a grant to have filmed Hitler Youth Documents in the Bundesarchiv of the German Republic, Koblenz, and to thank Drs. Kohte and Booms there for having the filming done. Mrs. Agnes Peterson, Curator of the Central and Western European Collections, Hoover Institution, Stanford California was of invaluable help to me, as she must be to everyone who does research there. The entire Hoover Library staff always proved knowledgeable and generous with its time and assistance.

I wish to thank the University of Southern California, for providing a generous research grant and summer fellowship from funds provided under the National Defense Education Act, which made possible the completion of this manuscript. My thanks to Mrs. Marina Scholl who served as my Italian-reading research assistant at USC and scanned many microfilm reels of *Osservatore Romano.* Herbert Luft, of the Heidelburg campus of Pepperdine College, carefully read the manuscript and checked some of my translations. Thanks also go to James Orville Smith, of Los Angeles for editing, to Mrs. Mitzi Wada, Torrance, California for typing the final draft, to Eleanore Humphrey of Glendale, California for preparing the index, and to Maynard T. Smith, Los Angeles, who guided the manuscript through these processes.

Special thanks go to my wife, Lee, who typed thousands of note cards, more drafts than I care to remember, and discussed every aspect of this work with me in its various stages of development.

Introduction

Chronologically, this study deals primarily with the period from the Nazi seizure of power to the Hitler Youth Law of December 1, 1936. It is a study of the conflict between the Hitler Youth (*Hitler Jugend*) and the Catholic youth organizations (especially the largest of these, the *Katholischer Jungmännerverband* or JMV) and between the much greater entities which stood behind both. Behind the Catholic youth organizations stood the power of the Catholic Church. Behind the Hitler Youth stood the Nazi regime with its enormous powers, powers which during the early years of the regime could not be exercised in a wholesale fashion without regard for foreign and domestic public opinion. I have attempted to examine the coercive pressures which Nazi totalitarianism brought to bear upon the Catholic youth organizations and to expand our knowledge of the youth organizations which held out longest against the total claims of that system.

In its earlier years, the Hitler Youth was little more than an S.A. for adolescents; in its last phase, it became a ponderous state organization for the physical education, disciplining, and indoctrination of all German youth. The years 1933-1936 were the transitional ones for the Hitler Youth, when it was much more than a party youth and yet, still less than a state youth. During this period, its totalitarian claims were expressed and largely realized. The HJ wished to deny to all other youth groups activities deriving either from the autonomous youth movement or from the gymnastic and sports associations. The principal obstacle to the totalitarian development of the Hitler Youth was the Catholic youth organizations, especially the largest, the JMV.

The Catholic youth organizations held out longest against the claims of the Hitler Youth because their position was protected. Pope Pius XI had a deep affection for and commitment to the Catholic youth organizations; he regarded them as providing a new indispensable method of Christian education and as the best defense against the religion of Blood and Soil which permeated the Hitler Youth. The method of Christian education developed in the Catholic youth groups

viii

combined Christian principles with the activities and group spirit of the *Wandervogel* and its successor of the 1920's, the *Bündische Jugend*. The continued existence in the Catholic youth organizations of activities absorbed from the free or autonomous youth movement became a major source of conflict between the church and state. There was no room for compromise between the total claims of the Hitler Youth to all youth activities outside of school and church and the Pope's determination not to surrender the extra-churchly activities of the Catholic youth organizations and transform all Catholic youth groups into sodalities.

Another source of strength for the youth organizations was the courage of the members. Their ability to hold to their organizations under great pressures probably owed something to religious factors, particularly the attitude of the Catholic Church toward suffering and martyrdom for the faith, but it also owed something to the sense of community developed within the youth groups. This combination of the personal support of the Pope and the determined resistance of youth leaders and members enabled the organizations to survive as effective groups for several years after the Nazi seizure of power.

In the end, the conflict was resolved by the application of a vast array of coercive powers to the Catholic youth. Individuals were placed at a disadvantage in seeking employment or admission to universities. Groups were forcibly restricted: in the summer of 1935 the Gestapo prohibited to Catholic youth organizations any extra-churchly activities and rigidly enforced the law. Beginning in 1936, one diocesan group after another was dissolved by police decree, allegedly for infractions of the prohibition. Police also took direct action against the central organization of the JMV. Several of its prominent leaders were arrested, and a few sent to prison. *Michael,* the principal publication of the JMV, and one of the financial mainstays of the organization, was suppressed by the Reich Press Chamber. The local finance office in Düsseldorf deprived the JMV headquarters of its exemptions, and imposed an enormous bill for taxes.

As pressure increased, the Church began to prepare against the time when the youth groups would be prohibited. From the summer of 1935, the Church had been working out a new basis for spiritual care for youth, and by June 1938 the JMV, fatigued and a skeleton of its former self, was willing to dissolve in an effort to save what property it could for the new program of spiritual care for youth. But in February 1939, before the JMV was able to carry out a voluntary dissolution, the Gestapo dissolved it and confiscated its goods.

In the end, the Catholic youth organizations were destroyed. But as long as they had continued to exist they had provided for their members moral and religious education of a special quality. The nature of this education, and the efforts to protect it against a very different sort of education, is the theme of this work.

CHAPTER ONE

Search and Rebellion

In the last decades of the nineteenth century, Germany became the strongest and most productive country in Europe. Yet, in the realm of political ideals, it remained poor. The libertarian ideals of the Enlightenment, which in France had gone into the making of the Revolution and the creation of the ideal of the free citizen, in the Revolution of 1848, in Germany, had gone down in defeat before the power of men who adhered to an older set of ideals: those of authority and submission. With the discrediting of libertarian ideals which might have given greater dignity to their lives, Germans came increasingly to worship power. The tendency was clearly inherent in German culture, but in the late nineteenth century it became explicit and crass. The French citizen may have identified with power no less than the German subject came to, but for the French, the strengthened state embodied revolutionary ideals; whereas the German's identification with the state's ascendancy was identification with the opponents of those revolutionary ideals. For the German subject, in a way, this meant identifying with his own act of submission.

To submit to power without seeing some good in it is destructive of personality. Germany saw the good; for Bismarck had forcefully achieved national liberation, unification and prestige, at least as dear to the men of 1848 as their libertarian and humanitarian goals. Yet, for all the satisfaction national pride provided, apparently something was still missing.

The notorious German emphasis on titles, so anomalous in the twentieth century, may be a symptom of a lack. When an individual puts great emphasis upon externals, he betrays that he has little faith in himself. It is significant that the German most likely to disintegrate in the concentration camps of the Nazi regime was the middle class pillar of the community, who in his normal life had put so much stock in various sorts of formalisms. The middle class, which in other states had so often been the spearhead of political reform, in Germany gained no such function and developed no corresponding social ideals. The average, secure citizen apparently developed little

1

sense of worth except that attested by titles of respect and function. Yet, in accepting the supreme importance of titles, the middle class German accepted a position of permanent inferiority to the noble, for no title of function could equal a title of nobility. Still, he could derive satisfaction from his superiority to the untitled classes, and, within his own class, he was superior to those with lesser titles or fewer of them.

Other symptoms of hollowness in German society were the mounting conflict between generations, and the rebellious protest of youth known as the youth movement. The two may be related; for both were primarily middle-class phenomena. One cause of the increasing severity of the conflict between generations during the latter part of the nineteenth century may lie in the changes brought about by Germany's rapid industrialization, perhaps, above all, in the changes within the middle class. It was this class which experienced the most immediate discontinuity in the occupational roles of fathers and sons. New occupations in trade or in technical fields were open to the middle class boy, and he was not as likely to follow in the footsteps of his father as was the son of the noble officer or, for other reasons, the son of the worker. In the new occupations, a father's experience was largely irrelevant, and his influence unneeded. Yet the socioeconomic facts cannot entirely account for the phenomenon: Germany's economic development was not sufficiently different from that of England or France to explain the depth and virulence of the clash between generations in Germany; nor account for the fact that in Germany alone an autonomous youth movement emerged. An explanation is needed which takes into account the difficulty the adolescent in Imperial Germany had in achieving a sense of purpose, of personal worth, and of identity.

Two psychoanalysts, Bruno Bettelheim and Erik Erikson, though approaching the conflict of generations from different angles, have analyzed the problem in terms which relate political ideas and values to the adolescent quest for identity. It is to be expected that these analysts, both of whom work with the young, should be concerned with the younger generation's search for identity. It is more surprising that both should attribute to political ideals such an important role in psychological maturation.

Erikson addressed himself directly to the problem in Germany, and ascribed the tension between fathers and sons to the older generation's lack of meaningful political ideals. Having no concept of political man, the German father lacked a concept of political maturity. Since the father had power but not ideals, his authority was not respected. He himself lacked a "true inner authority—that authority which results from an integration of cultural ideal and educational method." In the absence of such an inner authority, the "average German father, either habitually or in decisive moments, came to represent the habits and the ethics of the German top-sergeant and petty official, who would never be more, but was in constant danger of becoming less; and who had sold the birthright of a free man for a title and a life pension."[1]

Bettelheim was concerned primarily with American generations when he wrote:

"Old age is happiest when it can take youth up to the threshold of the good and the new and, like the mythical father of the West, point out the Promised Land to its children, saying: you and only you in a hard fight will have to make this your own; because what is handed down to you, what you have not won for yourselves, is never truly your own.

"Youth, on the other hand, is happiest when it feels it is fighting to reach goals that were conceived of but not realized by the generation before them. What the older generation urgently wished for itself, but had to acknowledge as the hope of the future—that is the legacy of youth. That the preceding generation wished to create such a better world makes it a worthy standard for youth. To come closer to achieving it through its own efforts proves to youth that it is gaining its own rich maturity."[2]

The German middle class lacked such a working relationship between its generations. The older generation lacked political ideals, it pointed to no promised land. In the youth movement, the younger generation sought to create its own ideals; but these, seemingly, had little to do with society at large. The youth group was a society in itself, and within it, the young felt a warmth of attachment they could not feel for their elders. The greater society was formal and rigid; the lesser one was warm and friendly. The adult world was increasingly urban, materialistic, competitive, and purposeful. The youth world sought the countryside, was adventurous, erotic in the broad sense, and served no purpose beyond itself. It was not a preparation for adult life, it was a rejection of adult life as it existed in Germany. The youth movement was not a political protest, however much a political vacuum in Germany had to do with provoking it, but a rebellion against a society in which youth could find little emotional satisfaction, and almost no moral inspiration. Thus, the young created a promised land of their own, apparently incongruent with social and political reality, developing their own values within, and explicitly confining them to the community of youth groups. They aimed to create a new form of man, but the form was elitist and insulated.

To use terminology borrowed from Max Weber and Ernest Troeltsch, the youth groups in their pre-war *Wandervogel* phase were "sects" like the Anabaptists of the sixteenth century.[3] A "sect" does not seek directly to transform the larger society, which is beyond its powers, but rejects that as evil and tries rather to form its own more nearly perfect society. That was the role the youth movement played. Within its cells it developed islands of values of a demanding and exalted nature which gave meaning to young lives. Its capacities for loyalty and idealism are attested by the appalling casualties former youth leaders suffered during the First World War: of 12,000 who went to war, 7,000 were killed. Of the total membership of the *Wandervogel,* one-fourth died in battle.[4] Significantly, their ideals had more relevance to a Germany at war than a Germany at peace. In more settled times, the younger generation had to come to terms with the values of the older; for the youth movement was without social goals, offered no program for the adult society, and had no direct effect upon it. The *Wandervogel* acknowledged no purpose beyond the development of a unique sort of individual, and the fostering of a unique sort of group experience which came with being out in nature with one's comrades.[5] In a manner of speaking, it fostered a horizontal attachment to one's comrades, but not a vertical one to the older generation and to the future reality. The sense of community was an end in itself, and its formation a deeply moving experience but an experience which had no issue. It affected the individual profoundly, but did not bind him to the past and the future. Viewed in this way, the youth movement contributed nothing to the solution of the problem which called it forth. As the boy became the man, he put away his childish ideals and entered the competition for money and status, retaining only a sense of warmth for his old comrades and a sense of guilt for having submitted to what he had once rejected.

CHAPTER TWO

Youth Movement and Youth Organizations

Wandervogel

The youth movement dates from 1896, when Herman Hoffman, a student at Berlin University, formed a group for the study of shorthand from students of the Steglitz Grammar School, located in a Protestant, middle class suburb on the outskirts of Berlin. Hoffman led his boys on hikes in the immediate region, and, then, in 1897, led them over the Harz mountains on a two week excursion. In 1897, they hiked to the Rhine, and in 1899, spent four weeks in the mountains of Bavaria. Hoffman completed his studies, and in January 1900, had a long talk with Karl Fischer, who was then nineteen. Fischer, who had been Hoffman's aide in the Bavarian expedition, now assumed leadership in the Steglitz circle. He led the group on more frequent excursions, fired it with enthusiasm, and gave it a model: the medieval itinerant scholar. He had great plans, and determined to set his group on a permanent basis. Conscious of the need for official toleration of its activities, on November 4, 1901, Fischer brought together four other youth leaders and five adult citizens, and together they established an association, the *"Wandervogel;* Committee for School Boys' Rambles." With this act, the youth movement formally began.

The *Wandervogel* fragmented almost from the start. As early as 1904, Fischer quarreled with three lesser leaders of the Steglitz group, withdrew, and founded a new group, the *Altwandervogel*. When Fischer moved to Halle to attend the university, Wilhelm Jansen succeeded him. Fischer's attempts to retain control of the *Altwandervogel* from Halle were unsuccessful; but Jansen soon had his own troubles, seceded from *Altwandervogel,* and founded still another group, the *Jungwandervogel*. Meanwhile, in 1906, Fischer had gone to China to perform his military service with a German naval batallion. He did not return to Germany until 1921. By then his role in the youth movement had been forgotten, but it owed much of its enthusiastic, undomesticated style to him.

5

Many *Wandervogel* groups sprang up during the years following Fischer's departure. They were products of the cities, especially those of central Germany. and throughout the youth movement's history there was an emphasis on escape from the city out into the beauties of nature. But, the most important feature of the youth movement was the deep sense of community the member derived from being together with his friends, especially when on a ramble.[1]

The groups varied immensely. Some were exclusively for boys; some admitted girls; and a few were separate organizations for girls. Peripheral causes, advocated by one group or another, included every-thing from alcoholic abstinence to nudism; but they all had in common their characteristic activities and their form of leadership, which was always by a person only slightly older than the others. The central activity of the groups was the long expedition, which took place during the summer. On holidays and weekends, they often made shorter excursions. At first, the *Wandervogel* met at school or in a member's home to plan rambles; but in time, the meetings themselves became important, and groups acquired a *Nest* or *Heim* as a meeting place, usually a shed or an old farmhouse on the outskirts of the city. There was much singing with all of these activities, and folk dancing in some groups. Although the youth movement produced no important art or literature, it did revive German folk songs and produced a good many songs of its own.

The members of a group (*Gruppe* or *Horde*) ranged from about twelve to nineteen years. Boys under twelve were unlikely to have the endurance for long rambles; those over nineteen usually left to attend universities or developed other interests. The size of groups ranged from as few as seven or eight to occasionally as many as twenty members; but the tendency was to keep the group compact and close in its attachments. The groups of a city were united in a *Ortsgruppe*, and the *Ortsgruppe* of a province belonged to a *Gau*. The various *Gaue* in turn were united in a *Bund*.

Between 1910 and 1913, the movement spilled over the borders of Germany into Switzerland and Austria. Older members, who went on to the universities, founded student groups which tried to keep something of the *Wandervogel* spirit. In 1913, leaders of those uni-versity groups proposed uniting the various youth and student groups under the name *Freideutsche Jugend*, and, in October 1913, staged a meeting of youth groups atop the Hohe Meissner, a peak laden with German legend. This meeting was the high point of the pre-war youth movement. From it came the Meissner formula, which in effect declared the intention of youth to shape their own lives.[2] But the plan for unity was never realized, and the partial unity of *Wandervogel* and student groups achieved under the name *Freideutsche Jugend* split into two wings as early as March 1914. Then, in July, came the war.

The youth movement throughout its history was middle class and elitist. Sons of nobles did not join because nobles still kept their distance from burghers. Sons of workers rarely joined because most *Wandervogel* groups were made up of schoolmates, and the working class was systematically excluded from secondary schools in Germany. The youth movement in its *Wandervogel* phase never numbered over 30,000; and in its later *bündische* phase, probably never over 60,000. Yet, its influence was far greater than its numbers indicate. It transformed the nature of youth work.

The two poles of youth work in Germany were the "youth movement" (*Jugendbewegung*) and "youth care" (*Jugendpflege*). The youth movement was the unique phenomenon which aimed at creating its own values, and its own communities of adolescents bound together by a special sort of experience. Youth care was the activity of adult organizations, such as churches, cultural associations, and political parties, whose immediate aim was to care for special interests of youth within the value scheme of the adult organization, and whose ultimate aim was to induct youth into full participation in the adult group. An example of an organization at this pole would be a Catholic young people's sodality concerned only with teaching young people the Catholic faith and encouraging them to receive the sacraments. In the 1920's, organizations of such a purely "youth care" sort became rarer. Many Catholic youth groups were transfixed by the romantic appeal of the youth movement and assumed youth movement activities and attitudes, while keeping safely within the context of the sponsoring adult organization.

Bündische Jugend

The transfer of youth movement spirit to confessional organizations was facilitated by changes occuring within the autonomous youth movement itself, which in the 1920's became much more disciplined and organized. The free, or autonomous, youth movement passed through two phases of development, the break between the phases coming with World War I. The sort of group represented by Karl Fischer's Steglitz ramblers dominated the period prior to the war. With the spirit of romantic escape buzzing in their minds, members of this type of group went off on excursions dressed in short leather breeches and blouses, guitars strung over their shoulders. Then came the war, and the continuity of the youth movement was snapped. One-fourth of the *Wandervogel* who went off to war, including the most important youth leaders, were killed. The veterans who returned were no longer boys, and their interests were likely to have changed. If they had not, the former soldiers found that their ideas conflicted with those of boys of fifteen or sixteen who had dominated the groups while they were away. Most important of all, the war had produced a new world, and the *Wandervogel* spirit was anomaly in it. A few groups, resembling the pre-war *Wandervogel* arose, but most of the new groups which arose in this period took on a new form.

The new era began with a dispute within the German Boy Scouts (*Pfadfinder*). Although the *Pfadfinder* had been organized in 1911, and before 1914 already counted 80,000 members, the scouts had had no influence upon the pre-war *Wandervogel*. The two were very different. Youth led the *Wandervogel*; adults led the scouts. The *Wandervogel* concentrated on rambles; the scouts on woodcraft and paramilitary training. The *Wandervogel* wore bizarre clothing and strolled; the scouts wore uniforms and marched. External disparity merely accented the wide divergence in goals and attitudes. The scouts presumably were in training as future full citizens of the larger society; the *Wandervogel* were citizens of a private world.

In 1920, some reformers broke away from the *Pfadfinder*, and their new group, the *Neupfadfinder,* hit upon a style which set the pattern for the many youth groups (*Bünde*) of the post-war period. The *Neupfadfinder* joined *Wandervogel* group spirit to scout discipline and civic responsibility, and fused them with a new romanticism of battle.

The new *Bünde*, which proliferated in this era, felt obliged to take a political stance, and that stance was usually *völkisch*. Even the

Wandervogel had not been able to avoid all political questions, though that was their intent. In the two years prior to the war, antisemites, who had hoped to make the *Wandervogel* politically conscious, found ways to provoke discussion of the "Jewish problem", a problem which touched youth groups directly whenever Jews applied for admission. What had been difficult to avoid before the war became impossible to avoid after the revolution in November 1918, and the subsequent social and political crises of the twenties. With politics and society in such flux, no one could be indifferent to the possible directions change might take, nor avoid having opinions about the possible alternatives.

The politicization of the youth movement took a variety of forms with the various *Bünde*. One extreme right wing group, the *Artamans,* started a back-to-the-soil movement designed to halt the influx of Polish agricultural laborers and keep Germans on the farm, a program later taken over by the Hitler Youth. Some *Bünde* cooperated with Free Corps in the early twenties. The *Freischar,* formed in 1926 by a merger of the *Neupfadfinder* and the *Altwandervogel,* took an academic approach to political questions and tried to analyze party programs and slogans. Although it had little enthusiasm for the Weimar republic, the *Freischar* found nothing to its taste on the right or the left and undertook to reform the existing government; in 1930, it supported what was intended to become a new party of the center, but with little success. There were other groups advocating several varieties of National Bolshevism, which was to reform German society, but remain free of international communism. How such a revolution was to be implemented was at best unclear.

The images and associated fantasies of youth were striking indicators of the direction of change in political awareness, and the changes there represented a profound alteration of values. The *Wandervogel* ideal had been the itinerant scholar; the *Bünde* idealized the warrior: first, the medieval knight; later, in some groups, the Samurai and the Cossack. By nature these images loaned themselves more to the nationalist extreme right than to the left or center. After 1921, there was no left wing in the free youth movement, in any case; National Bolshevism having more in common with right extremism than with communism. The image of the warrior certainly had little to do with the political center, which would have required an image both more practical and prosaic.

The National Socialist youth easily surpassed most of the *Bünde* in the degree of its politicization, and, especially in its early years, was more an SA (*Sturm Abteilung*) for adolescents than an heir of the *Wandervogel*. Still, it did have some of the characteristics of a *Bund*. The young National Socialists wore uniforms, marched, and had war games like many of the *Bünde*. In fact, before 1926, it was not always clear whether the party-sponsored SA for boys, or one of the far right *Bünde* such as the *Schilljugend* was the real National Socialist youth group. Further proof of some common elements between the HJ and the youth movement was provided in 1931, when the Hitler Youth incorporated a *Bund* for younger boys, the *Jungvolk,* which in time became an indispensable part of the Nazi youth apparatus. *Bündische* spirit is even supposed to have lived on for a time in the *Jungvolk,* until it attracted the attention of the HJ leadership and the former youth movement leaders were purged. In the long run, Hitler Youth values and *Wandervogel* spirit proved incompatible. The thoroughly politicized HJ could never tolerate the spirit of autonomy and adolescent rebellion which was the essence of the youth movement.

National Socialist Youth

The origins of the National Socialist Youth Organization date back to February 1922, but the history of the early years is extremely confused. In a letter of June 8, 1937 to Rudolf Hess, Baldur von Schirach, leader of the Hitler Youth since 1931, refused to recognize that there had been any National Socialist youth organization preceeding the formal establishment of the Hitler Youth, under that name, by Adolf Hitler at the Weimar party rally in July 1926. Schirach's excuse was rather lame: if he recognized one precursor, he would have to recognize all sorts of other groups as precursors too.[3] There is some truth in that, but the Nazi party *Hauptarchiv* historian, investigating the origins of the Hitler Youth, believed that Schirach objected less to recognition of precursors to the Hitler Youth than that he balked at accepting the first leader of the National Socialist youth Adolf Lenk. Whatever Schirach's reasons may have been, it is clear that a National Socialist youth organization existed from as early as 1922, although at times there was confusion as to whether Lenk's group, or one or another of the right wing *Bünde* was the true National Socialist youth organization. The National party leadership was little concerned about the matter anyway. After all, boys could not vote.

The first movement toward the establishment of a party youth organization came on February 25, 1922 when Adolf Hitler, in a circular letter, ordered the establishment of a youth division, and charged the leadership of the SA with organizing it. On March 8, 1922, the Nazi party newspaper, *Völkischer Beobachter*, issued an appeal for the founding of a *Jugendbund* of the NSDAP. That same month the statutes of the *Jugendbund* were drawn up. The youth organization was designated as the "rallying place of any comrade under 18 years of age who wishes to enter the *Sturmabteilung* of the NSDAP on his 18th birthday". The National Socialist youth organization was long to remain a mere youth auxiliary of the SA.

On May 13, 1922, the charter meeting of the *Jugendbund* was held in the *Bürgerbraukeller* in Munich, at which there were speeches by Adolf Hitler, Lt. Hans Ulrich Klintzsch, founder and leader of the SA, and one Gustav Adolf Lenk, youth leader of the new organization. There were 23 charter members. Within a year, however, Lenk had a structure of 54 *Ortsgruppen* and claimed about 2,000 members. During 1923, the organization was differentiated into the *Jungsturm,* for the older members; the *Jugend* for the younger boys; a girls division; and even a "National Socialist *Wandervogel*." Lenk claimed that by November 1923 he had 16,000 young people under his leadership.[4]

On November 9, 1923, Lenk called out the Munich *Jungsturm* groups to take part in the National Socialist "Revolution", and about 200 young National Socialists took possession of the war ministry.[5] With the collapse of the *putsch,* the youth organization, like the NSDAP, was banned. On November 28, Lenk was arrested and imprisoned in Landsberg fortress. Released on December 24, he set about establishing the *Grossdeutsche Jugendbewegung*. On October 15, 1924, he was again arrested, and held for eight weeks, while an investigation of his activities proceeded. He was released shortly before Christmas, on the condition that he report daily to the police.

For some reason, the period of Lenk's confinement seems to have been his undoing. In a letter of April 16, 1924, he complained to a friend that during that period certain party members had spread lies about him. He did not specify what "lies", and his record is at best a clouded one. In June 1924, he had been found guilty of stealing postage stamps from the *Völkische Presse,* and fined sixty RM. The *Hauptarchiv* investigator turned up a rumor that Lenk had been an informer for the Munich *Post.* A stray document from the *Hauptarchiv* files, labeled "Extract from the Position Report No. 28 of April 18, 1925", accuses Lenk of having less interest in collecting youth than in collecting dues. It also claimed that the youth organization recognized in *völkische* circles was the *Schilljugend,* set up by Gerhard Rossbach. The report alleged that the group led by the "cabinet maker" Adolf Lenk, in spite of a great deal of propaganda in the *völkische* press, had few followers, since it lacked the support of Hitler and other *völkische* leaders. A few days earlier, Rossbach had published an article on the *Schilljugend* in *Völkischer Beobachter,* the offical party organ.[6] Because of his record; or because his enemies were in the ascendency, or both, on April 22, 1925, Adolf Lenk resigned as leader of the National Socialist youth movement. Later, he was to claim that he had relinquished his position because his "frightful overwork in the year 1924" had undermined his health.[7] But in his letter to *Völkischer Beobachter* of April, 1925, in which he spelled out his reasons for resigning, he said nothing about health. Rather, he complained that his financial position no longer permitted him to offer his services, and that he was misunderstood by the men around Hitler, and by the administration of the party, who knew nothing about a youth movement. After pledging his loyalty to Adolf Hitler, Lenk asked for contributions to help cover a 200 RM deficit in the treasury.

Lenk's letter was referred to Rossbach by Edmund Heines, a leader of the *Schilljugend...* Rossbach advised the party leadership not to publish Lenk's letter, but merely to state he had departed from the youth movement. Rossbach continued that he did not think it advisable, if one were to mention the matter in the press, that Hitler should take an active position regarding the *Schilljugend.* Rather, it should be said that Hitler was pleased with the activity of the youth movement in general and from the "*völkische* and defense educational" standpoints particularly approved the work of the *Schilljugend,* because it strove for cooperation with other youth groups in the furthering of military training.[8] On May 13, a short notice appeared in *Völkischer Beobachter:*

Attention!

After the departure of Mr. G. A. Lenk, I wish to refer all questions concerning the youth movement to the leadership of the Schilljugend, addressed to the attention of Mr. Edmund Heines, Munich, Schellingstrasse 98.

Munich, 6 May, 1925

Signed: Adolf Hitler

This proved to be only an interlude. Lenk claims that when he heard of the appointment of Heines, whom he did not regard as a suitable youth leader, he wrote to Hitler recommending his own best subordinate, Kurt Gruber, who had been very successful in organizing National Socialist youth in Saxony. Lenk did regard Gruber as one of his best youth leaders and as a personal friend, it is quite possible that he did recommend him. However, Lenk claims that he wrote to Hitler on March 16, 1925, which would be well before Hitler's order to refer youth matters to the leadership of the *Schilljugend,* indicating that Lenk's recommendation had no effect. Nonetheless, Gruber did emerge in the following year as the recognized leader of the National Socialist youth organization, when Hitler commissioned him at the Nazi Party rally of July 1926 to lead the *Hitler Jugend* (Hitler Youth), as the organization was christened.

Gruber apparently had already won informal recognition, for as early as October, 1925, he had staged a leaders' conference at his home base in Plauen, Saxony. But, his appointment by Hitler at the party rally in Weimar in July, 1926 did not mean that his struggle to gain recognition for the National Socialist youth organization was at an end. The history of the Hitler Youth throughout Gruber's tenure is the story of an organization starved by the party leadership for funds and recognition. It was 1928 before Gruber could set up a small administrative office in a cellar in Plauen. As late as October 1932, Schirach still complained of the "regrettable fact that the National Socialist party had neither money nor essential ideological support for its youth." There was scarcely one HJ leader who had even minimal financial support, and Schirach felt that the youth organization was regarded as a "fifth wheel."[9]

Nevertheless, under Gruber, the youth organization was beginning to become a significant arm of the Nazi party. Its usefulness grew, not in terms of membership, which remained ridiculously small in comparison to the adult membership of the NSDAP; but because its leaders staged great demonstrations which could leave no doubt in the minds of Nazis, or others, that a National Socialist youth movement did in fact exist. At the Nuremberg party rally in August of 1927, Gruber assembled nearly a thousand Hitler Youth. At the fourth party rally, called again at Nuremberg in August 1929, Gruber brought the *bündische* "tent camp" into politics. Approximately 3,500 *Hitlerjugend* participated in the camp, and in a parade before Hitler. Schirach brought the tactic to a new height in October, 1932, when the Hitler Youth held a Reich Youth Day in Potsdam. Approximately 40,000 participants were expected, but 70,000 appeared, probably reflecting the electoral successes of the Nazi party. This produced a certain amount of chaos, but the monster demonstration was a great success. *Hitlerjugend* paraded for hours before the outstretched arm of Adolf Hitler. Not that all of these 70,000 were dues-paying members of the Hitler Youth, for in this time of economic depression, not all who would like to have joined could afford to pay dues. The membership of the three National Socialist youth organizations, (Hitler Youth, *Jungvolk* in the Hitler Youth, and the *Bund Deutscher Mädel* in the Hitler Youth), was a mere 42,306 in January 1932.[10]

During the years immediately preceding Schirach's tenure, the HJ improved its structural and administrative position, and gained greater reputation within the National Socialist party.

Under the "Guidelines for the Relations between the NSDAP and Hitler Youth", drawn up at Weimar, on December 5, 1926, the National Socialist youth organization had remained as much an auxiliary of the SA, and stepchild of the party as before its change of name. The leader of the HJ was required "to regulate all important affairs and difficulties of the HJ, only after having obtained the permission of the corresponding NSDAP leadership (von Pfeffer)." (Von Pfeffer was chief of the S.A.) Gruber was able to obtain a measure of autonomy for the Hitler Youth in the "Guidelines between the Hitler Youth and Party" and the "Guidelines between Hitler Youth and SA," both signed in Munich on April 23, 1929. By these two agreements, the status of the youth leader and his administrative office was elevated, and some limit was set to the powers of the SA over the youth organization. Gruber had requested a position which would give him more influence in party deliberations touching upon the youth organization, and this was reflected in a provision that the Hitler Youth leader could participate in meetings of the party leadership when they dealt with matters relevant to his sphere of activity. The Hitler Youth leadership was authorized to correspond directly with the various departments of the party leadership; and the departments of the Reich party leadership were to correspond directly with the central office of the Hitler Youth Reich leadership in Plauen. SA men were ordered not to meddle in the internal administration of the Hitler Youth. Hitler Youth were not required individually to participate in SA demonstrations, but only when the HJ was called out as a group, as agreed between the SA and HJ leaders. Finally, Gruber won acceptance of his projected Reich Hitler Youth Day, to take place within the Reich Party Day. The guidelines guaranteed authorization for mass public demonstrations of the HJ, and it was under such authorization that Gruber led his triumphant march of *Hitlerjugend* before the Führer at the Nuremberg party rally in August of that year.

Two other steps Gruber took were important to the development of the Hitler Youth organizational structure. On March 27, 1931, the *Jungvolk,* a rightwing *Bund,* was incorporated into the Hitler Youth as the *"Jungvolk* in the Hitler Youth," and charged with organizing boys between the ages of seven and fifteen. *Jungvolk* members over fifteen, who were not made leaders of the *Jungvolk* in the Hitler Youth, were to be taken into Hitler Youth proper; and those over eighteen were to go into the SA. In the beginning, the membership in this lower age classification was quite small. In January 1932, when there were 42,306 members in the three National Socialist youth groups, 37,304 of these were in the Hitler Youth, and only 3,267 in the *Jungvolk.* The remaining 1,735 were in the *"Bund Deutscher Mädel* in the Hitler Youth"*, which originated in 1930 through a union of several girls' auxiliaries to the HJ. The relative membership figures reflect the persistent character of the HJ as the adolescent's SA. The HJ was not yet a genuine party youth, much less the state youth it was to become. As the Nazi party came to consolidate its hold over

German state and society, it found a wider role for the *Jungvolk* and BDM.

In October 1931, Gruber, who apparently was not in the best of health, was appointed to the Youth Committee of the NSDAP. Adrian von Renteln, who had organized the National Socialist *Schüler-bund* (for secondary school boys) in 1929, was called to lead the Hitler Youth as well. Baldur von Schirach, who had succeeded to the leadership of the National Socialist *Studentenbund* (for university students) in 1928, retained that office; and, in addition, was appointed to head a newly created office in the SA leadership, Reich Youth Leader of the NSDAP. Schirach was directly responsible to the chief of staff of the SA.

On assuming his office as Hitler Youth leader in November 1931, Renteln found that the local youth leaders were lackadaisical about sending in their periodic reports, and the whole organization was anarchic: the individual *Gaue* went their own way (the "HJ in this was like a miniature of the NSDAP"); he even found a special SS within the HJ; and in the Reich Youth Leadership, he found a number of independent advisory experts and officials who sent out instructions on their own authority, and without any guarantee that they would be followed. Renteln set out to tidy up the lines of administration, and to recruit new members for the Hitler Youth. His tenure was short, however, for in May and June 1932, Hitler placed all of the National Socialist youth groups under Baldur von Schirach, and made him an official leader in the Reich Leadership of the NSDAP. Renteln was appointed to the economic division of the party, and Schirach took over direct leadership of the HJ, thus coming into direct control of all three youth organizations of the party. The evolution was capped on June 1, 1933, when Hitler, who now led the German state as well as the Nazi party, gave new power to Schirach, Reich Youth Leader of the NSDAP, by appointing him to a new office, Youth Leader of the German Reich. The story of the next few years can be viewed as an attempt to make the two titles synonymous.

Schirach attacks the Bünde

The success of the Hitler Youth was directly bound up with the success of the NSDAP. By the time Hitler was appointed chancellor on January 30, 1933, Schirach estimated that the Hitler Youth numbered around one million. Approximately a year later, the figure was nearer three million, and the HJ was on the way to becoming Germany's only youth organization. During the spring and summer of 1933, the Hitler Youth abolished all party youth organizations which failed to dissolve themselves; incorporated or dissolved nearly every autonomous youth organization; and, by the end of 1933, had begun incorporating the Evangelical youth groups.

The story of these months is hardly edifying. In an effort to retain their corporate identities and retain possession of their homes, work camps, and other properties, some of the *Bünde* hastened to win the favor with the new state. The leaders of the *Deutsche Freischar* were the first to act. On May 8, 1933, three days after the Reichstag election, but two weeks before the new Reichstag voted Hitler full powers, the *Freischar* leaders announced that they were joining the Nazi party and expressed the hope that the other *Bündische Jugend* would follow their example.

Schirach, for one, was not impressed. On April 5, 1933, he sent an armed group of Hitler Youth to occupy the business offices of the Reich Committee of German Youth Organizations, a clearing house of information which was the point of contact for the numerous and varied organizations for youth in Germany. On April 10, he sent another detachment to take over the Reich Association for German Youth Hostels. Schirach used the records of the Reich Committee to ascertain the size of all German youth associations and to obtain the names of their leaders.

The object of Schirach's next attack was a conglomerate union of autonomous groups which had sought to escape incorporation into the Hitler Youth by placing themselves under the leadership of Admiral von Trotha, a friend of President von Hindenburg. The Admiral had led a short lived union of some of the *Bünde* in 1930, and at the end of March 1933, the *Freischar* and other *Bünde* placed themselves under his leadership. The new union, the *Grossdeutsche Jungenbund,* proclaimed its loyalty to National Socialist principles, but objected to Schirach and those who wanted a "fascist youth organization instead of the German Youth Group."[11] On April 15, the executive of the new organization resolved to integrate this new *Bund* with the National

Socialist movement. Early in May, the leader of the *Freischar* announced the consequences of the *Freischar's* confession of loyalty to the National Socialist state: anyone who had no place in the National Socialist movement, likewise was excluded from the *Freischar*—in other words: Jews and Marxists were no longer members. He made the *Gau* leaders of the organization responsible for the execution of this order.

Meanwhile, Schirach was staging demonstrations against the *Grossdeutsche Bund*. Still trying to maintain some sort of separate existence, the *Bund* next asked to join the Hitler Youth as a group. Hitler refused the request on June 1, 1933.

Schirach thought his organization unequal to the task of dissolving the *Grossdeutsche Bund*, and discussed the matter with Hitler. On June 17, 1933, Hitler gave him the powers he needed by appointing him Youth Leader of the German Reich. In a typically Nazi mixing of party and state functions, the Reich Youth Leader, as such, stood under the Minister of Interior, Frick. The purpose of the arrangement was to allow Schirach to use the power of the state without having to maintain a bureaucracy within the Hitler Youth. Schirach, as Youth Leader of the German Reich, was allowed to appoint to the interior ministry's youth division in each German state, an official to execute his orders.

On the day of his appointment as Youth Leader of the German Reich, Schirach used his new powers to dissolve the *Grossdeutsche Bund*. Approximately 15,000 members of the organization were at camp when HJ, SA, and police surrounded them and took them away in trucks. That same day, Hitler Youth details invaded the business offices and Youth Homes of all of the larger *Bünde*. Admiral von Trotha protested to Hitler and to President von Hindenburg, but to no avail. The era of the *Bünde* was at an end.

"What was once called the German youth movement is dead," wrote Schirach in 1934;[12] but the spirit of the youth movement proved more difficult to eradicate than its organizations, and even a few of those maintained a clandestine existence. At the core of the *Wandervogel* spirit, was an act of rebellion against, and escape from the tedium of a rigid, materialistic, adult-dominated society. But the Hitler

Youth could tolerate neither juvenile escapism, nor personal revolt. Schirach, who detested the *Bünde* for their lack of political consciousness, their elitism and romanticism, considered the Hitler Youth, in its aspect as a focus of political force, far more responsive to the deepest needs of German youth. For Schirach, as for Hitler, the role and end of politics were those of the developed, emotional pseudo-religion; politics became politics in the full totalitarian sense: the one party state and its inverse morality poised against free apathy, rational uncertainty, and spontaneity. Within that framework, any action not rooted in social and national utility had to be regarded as essentially immoral. "A youth group has a right to exist only if its purpose is directed for the nation," Schirach wrote, or put another way, "the symbol of the *Bünde* was the ramble, the symbol of the HJ is the Reich Trades Competition."[13] Since if everything were to be valued in terms of social and national utility, there could be no room for random, personal, or eccentric actions, Schirach found it necessary not only to suppress the *Bünde,* but to interdict certain individual and/or spontaneous actions within the Hitler Youth itself. An excursion was a social act. Authorized by Hitler Youth leaders, and performed in uniform, it was a social good. But a ramble out of uniform, partially in uniform, or in "fantastic outfits and costumes," was an evil, and was made a punishable offense. "Youth must be led by youth,"[14] but led according to regulations.

As early as November 2, 1932, the Social Advisor of the HJ, in order to establish some control over Hitler Youth who were wandering about the country, required that they have an authorized "Wander Card."[15] That was a signpost for the future. The first serious step toward the suppression of random activity was taken during the Easter season in 1935, when the HJ staff leader, Lauterbacher, published the following statement in the Hitler Youth *Verordnungsblatt*[16]

HJ, *Jungvolk,* and BDM on Excursions:

During the Easter season, in all parts of Germany one meets wandering groups of boys or girls who stroll through the region in fantastic outfits and costumes. Inquiries have revealed that for the most part they are members of confessional youth groups or former members of Bünde, now forbidden. Unfortunately, however, members of HJ, Jungvolk, and BDM have also been seen under way either in individually-invented, special getups or half in civilian clothes. The [Hitler Youth leaders] are responsible for the HJ also on excursions and wanderings, which can only be regarded as minor service [kleindienst]. Members of the youth groups are forbidden to undertake wanderings and excursions in anything other than their prescribed uniforms.

"The Patrol Service of the HJ. . . .is prepared, in common with the police, to patrol in specially known wandering regions, on streets,—youth hostels, and so forth, from Pentecost [Whitsuntide] on. Members of the HJ who in the future are found on excursions and wanderings without the prescribed identity card, and clothed in other than the prescribed manner, will be punished accordingly. It is self evident that no colored neckerchiefs and such may be worn with the prescribed clothing. The leaders of the HJ and BDM are responsible not only for discipline inside the HJ, but are also obligated to protect Germany with all brutality and force from wild Wander groups strolling around, whether they belong to the HJ or have their base in confessional groups. Foreigners traveling to Germany this summer also will meet with greater discipline and order in the wandering regions, and especially on the streets.

Signed Lauterbacher.

Apparently, Lauterbacher's first warning had little effect, for he returned to the matter on May 9, 1935:[17]

"Wandering HJ:

The Bann and Jungbann leaders are notified for the last time that they are answerable for all excursions undertaken by the young people of their units. Reports from throughout the Reich are already piling up that wandering groups of Hitler Youth and Jungvolk are on the road who: 1) do not satisfy the general regulations concerning order and discipline and, 2) attempt to beg their way from village to village. This is to inform the whole subordinate leadership, once more, that the Reich Youth Leadership expressly forbids going on excursions without the necessary funds. Leaders, who in the future, are encountered with traveling groups who do not satisfy the regulations will eventually be punished with expulsion from the Hitler Youth.

Signed Lauterbacher.

The Hitler Youth Patrol Service, which was formed during the spring of 1935, received as its first major assignment the patrolling of hostels, streets, and regions favored by wandering groups.[18] Members of the Hitler Youth were obligated to show their identity cards, provide personal data, and obey the orders of the Patrol on demand. The Patrol was instructed that it had no right to detain, or question other youth groups. Nevertheless, the Patrol leader in a courteous manner should find out to what youth organization a particular wandering group belonged, and who was leading the excursion. He should note the number of participants, their average age, and their objective. This information, along with his impression of their discipline, or lack of it, was to be written up in a short report and sent on to the local *Bann* office. There, a comprehensive report would be drawn up, and sent to the next highest office.

Apparently, the efforts to maintain some sort of control over rambles was not very successful, and in October 1935, Lauterbacher explicitly made excursions a part of Hitler Youth service, and made the individual *Hitler Jugend* on a ramble subject to HJ discipline.[19]

"Wandering HJ:

Various offenses of the past year compel the following regulation:

The excursion belongs to the service of the HJ, and its organizations. Basically, therefore, it is always undertaken by the group. But even if a member of the HJ goes on a ramble, either alone, or with a few comrades, due to special circumstances— and this must always be regarded as exceptional— he is still in service; therefore in the future no excursion it to be made except in uniform. Only school excursions by class clubs are excepted.

The Patrol Service has instructions to ascertain the identity of members of the Hitler Youth who appear on excursions in fantastic uniforms, or half uniforms, and to report to the proper authorities.

Signed Lauterbacher.

So much for youth movement spirit in the HJ. In July 1935, the Gestapo set up a special section to keep surveillance over former leaders of the *Bünde* and had local offices of the Gestapo prepare lists of such persons. The ban against the *Bünde* was repeated in February 1936, then again in March 1937, and finally in July 1939. As late as May 1939, a circular letter of the Gestapo advised all branches to be on the lookout for *bündische* hikers, small groups of which apparently continued to exist despite the harsh penalties facing them if they were caught. But all in all, in 1934 Schirach was justified, if a bit premature, in asserting that the youth movement was dead. Only the Catholic youth organizations stood in the way, as the Reich Youth Leader said, "setting the 'I' of their groups against the 'We' of our community."[20]

Catholic Youth

The Catholic youth organization, which in spirit and activity stood closest to the *Wandervogel,* was *Quickborn.* This organization had its origin in an abstinence group for students in the secondary schools. It was united into the *Kreuzbund* with the abstinence organization for Catholic working boys, *Jungborn.* Both the organizations that came to comprise *Quickborn* were of strictly youth care nature, and a boy could easily belong to both the *Wandervogel* and *Quickborn*, without ever thinking of them as being related in any way. But three priest leaders of *Quickborn* in Silesia decided that to combat the student-style of life, which called for the consumption of the "bringer of joy," alcohol, they would have to substitute some joys of their own which would appeal to the young. Each of the priests brought something distinct to the combination. For one, the joy was rambling; for the second, singing; and for the third, a "joy in the Lord" like that of St. Francis.

When the groups of young Silesians began to ramble, they came into contact with the *Wandervogel,* and as a result of the experience adopted the dress, activities, and much of the spirit of the autonomous youth movement. In 1919, *Quickborn* took as its center, Castle Rothenfels, and from there spread over the boundaries of Silesia into Upper Silesia, Berlin, Westphalia, and Niederrhein.[21]

Quickborn maintained a creative tension of disparate elements. It was church-sponsored, but led by youth. Each small group of about fifteen was led by one of the members, but advised on moral and religious questions by a clerical "friend," who did not attempt to determine the group's activities. The separate groups for boys and girls did not wander together, but they did hold joint regional meetings, which were an interesting combination of camping, games, folk singing, and group dancing, combined with religious observances and serious moral discussions.

Quickborn apparently provided a means of expression for youth partly freed from adult domination. The youth engaged in activities which interested them, while clerical advisors inserted into the mixture religious activities of a sort which appealed to youth. The clerics not only countenanced the tacit rejection of adult society implied in the youth movement, but shared some of that spirit themselves, sensing in the movement a need to flee the "materialism" of adult German society and seeing in the youth organization an instrument for developing internal controls, and spiritual depth in the young person.[22]

By the early 1930's, *Quickborn* had 352 local groups and a total of 32,529 members. More important, *Quickborn* provided the channel through which *Wandervogel* style and activities passed to the other Catholic youth organizations.

The *Neudeutschland Bund* was the next Catholic youth organization to be influenced by the spirit of the youth movement. The organization originated in 1919 by order of the Archdiocese of Cologne as a mere club for school boys. By 1922, it had spread to other dioceses in northern Germany, numbering about 25,000 members, and was well on its way to becoming a large, and uninspired organization. Then, the ferment of change generated by the youth movement was introduced into *Neudeutschland*. Sometime around 1921, Pastor Johannes Zender, who, in 1922, became *Neudeutschland's* leader, decided with another pastor to lead twenty group members on a hike to Castle Rothenfels to attend a conference of 1500 *Quickborn* boys and girls. Here, *Neudeutschen* found a spirit very different from their own, and they were greatly impressed. "Here, one lived in a conscious sense of community and responsibility. . . ;" while, with the *Neudeutschen*, "one was still a grammer school boy, who let himself be led, and left all responsibility to the leader."[23]

Pastor Zender was not alone in being influenced by the *Quickborn,* and the spirit of the youth movement. The general meeting of the *Neudeutschen* in August 1921, turned into a hubbub over proposals to limit to an advisory role the activities of the clerical religion teachers who led the groups. Eventually, the organization worked out, at least in theory, a cooperative leadership by the youth leader and the priest. Meanwhile, youth movement influence continued to be felt in *Neudeutschland.* In 1922, the organization acquired the ruins of a castle, and the annual meeting of *Neudeutschland* held here that same year looked very much like a typical autonomous youth gathering.

In 1922, the original leader of the *Bund* died, and Pastor Zender was appointed in his place. The Fulda Conference of bishops had designated Cardinal Schulte, archbishop of Cologne, as the protector of *Neudeutschland,* and Pastor Zender was eager to discuss youth activities with the cardinal. The latter apparently had little interest in the matter. He confined himself to ordering Pastor Zender to strengthen the influence of the secular clergy in the *Bund*, and to limit the influence of the ordinary clergy, an order which Zender disobeyed, picking youth leaders where he found them, and ending up with a good many Jesuits in the organization. Neither at this, nor at any later time did Zender receive any significant help from Cardinal Schulte in his tasks.[24]

In 1923, the tensions between the youth movement, per se, and religious tendencies were crystallized in a new program which resolved to use the youth movement as a way to Christ. This Hirshberg program announced one major goal: to create a new form of life in Christ. There were to be two means to this goal. One was the youth movement. Through it, would be developed sound and loyal young men with an appreciation of the natural side of life expressed through their joy in song, wandering, play, and love for homeland and *Volk*. Within their groups, they would learn to act independently and creatively. They would be bound to their groups by a sense of community based, not on mere congeniality, but on brotherly love.

The second means to achieve the new form of life in Christ was for those young men to deepen their Catholicity, and their understanding of Christ through holding Him as a Model, through veneration of His mother, through receiving the Eucharist, practice of the liturgy, and participation in religious retreats and other devotional regimes.

The immediate result of the Hirshberg program was a sudden drop in membership. The demands were very high, and could be met only by an elite. On the other hand, the incorporation of the youth movement alienated many clerical religion teachers who had led the original *Neudeutschland,* and wanted nothing to do with the spirit of youth movement. They withdrew, as did several thousand of the rank and file. Lesser losses came the following year when other groups seceded because they wanted still more of the *Quickborn* pattern. By the beginning of 1925, *Neudeutschland* was down to 13,000 members. But, it grew steadily thereafter, and, on the eve of the Nazi seizure of power, claimed 21,472 members, or one-third of Germany's Catholic secondary school students.

Neudeutschland developed a much less buoyant, and exuberant tone than *Quickborn.* Members were rigidly selected, and their sense of religious dedication was almost monastic. It was an unwritten law that no one who smoked, drank, went out with girls, or danced was a true *Neudeutscher.* Many members went on to become priests, or members of orders—at one period as many as one-half of the *Neudeutschen* graduating from secondary school applied.[25]

The Catholic youth movement coincided with a European-wide ferment within the Catholic Church and furthered it by taking up the liturgical movement, itself a part of that broader religious ferment. It is not surprising that the "community mass" struck a harmonic chord in the youth groups with their strong sense of community. *Quickborn* was the first to be affected, coming in contact with the liturgical movement through the Benedictine monks. The *Neudeutschen,* first participating in a "community mass" at their annual meeting in 1924, and thereafter carrying it with them wherever they went, prepared the way. The *Jungmännerverband* spread the practice to a far greater audience, and printed over one million missals for use in reciting the liturgy.[26] The spread of the liturgical movement in Germany was chiefly the work of the youth organizations,[27] through whose agency the liturgy was brought to Catholic youth, and through the youth to their parents.

By far the largest Catholic youth organization, and the one upon which this study focuses, was the *Jungmännerverband* (JMV). The remote origins of the *Jungmännerverband* date back to 1896, when in Mainz, four sodalities or "congregations," as they were called, united their 40,000 members, and took the name *Katholischer Jungmännerverband Deutschlands.* By 1908, the JMV had 140,000 members, by 1918, 342,000; and by 1930, 387,000. Following a successful recruiting campaign during 1932, in 1933, the membership over fourteen years of age stood at 365,000; less than the 1930 figure, but actually representing a relative gain when the declining birth rate of the war years is taken into account[28] The strength of the JMV lay in the predominantly Catholic industrial regions of the Rhineland.[29]

The *Jungmännerverband* had a rather complex organization. In the first place, it was divided horizontally into three age group classifications: *Jungschar,* (to age 14), *Jungenschaft,* (14 - 18); and *Jungmannschaft,* (over 18 years of age). All three shared the PX insignia taken from the Greek letters signifying "Christ". The youngest group, the *Jungschar,* wore a common uniform consisting of blue blouses and short pants. The JMV census of 1933 indicated a *Jungschar* membership of 105,800, and a *Jungenschaft* membership of 146,483; while the *Jungmannschaft* numbered 218,514, for a total membership of 470,800. Totaling the figures of the *Jungschar* (105,800) and *Jungenschaft* (146,483), we find that in 1933, there were nearly a quarter of a million members of the JMV who were fair game for Hitler Youth recruiting.

In addition to being organized horizontally by age groups, a large percentage of the members of the JMV was also organized vertically into specialized "communities," with a total membership of 253,471. Assuming that the members of the JMV over 21 years of age were not likely to belong to these communities, possibly as much as 70 per cent of the membership of the JMV, 21 years of age or under, were enrolled in one or another of the specialized communities. The point is important, for the specialized groups were those most likely to have felt the influence of the *Bündische Jugend.* That put them into direct conflict with the Hitler Youth, which had little quarrel with sodalities, but which intended to drive all competing youth organizations off the streets and the playing fields.

The larger specialized communities, in addition to the PX monogram shared by the JMV in general, had their own particular insignia, uniforms, and banners. The largest specialized community was *Deutsche Jugendkraft* (DJK), which originated in 1920, and by 1933, reached a total of 148,150 members. A rather clear indication of the activities of the DJK is a list of its possessions in that year: it owned 387 gymnasiums; 1,229 playing fields; fourteen tennis courts; 47 swimming pools; 23 rifle ranges; and 11 boat houses. In its activities then, the DJK probably owed more to *Turnvater Jahn* than to Karl Fischer; it was less related to the *Wandervogel* than to the popular German gymnastics groups, mass organizations whose membership exceeded that of the autonomous youth movement several times over. Nonetheless, the DJK had *bündische* characteristics. Its basic unit was a group of fifteen and its members wore gray-green uniforms.

The next largest specialized community was the *Sturmschar,* which was founded in 1929 as an organization of secondary school boys, and in 1933, had 23,040 members. The *Sturmschar* wore a uniform consisting of a silver-gray shirt, and black trousers. This group, whose most cherished activity was the ramble, closely patterned itself upon the youth movement; there was indeed intense rivalry between this organization and *Neudeutschland,* whose leaders regarded the *Sturmschar* as an invader of their province. The common youth movement core of these two organizations and *Quickborn* is illustrated by the way in which *Quickborn* eventually merged into the *Sturmschar.* First, *Quickborn* joined with a splinter group from *Neudeutschland* to form a new group, the *Deutschmeister,* whose membership consisted primarily of secondary school and university students; probably as a precaution against the fate which befell the autonomous youth groups, in October 1933, the *Deutschmeister* joined the JMV as a specialized organization, and finally on June 29, 1934, merged into the *Sturmschar.*

Two other specialized groups within the JMV were the *Junglandbewegung,* and the *St. Georgs Pfadfinderschaft.* By 1933, the *Junglandbewegung,* founded in 1928 as an organization of farm boys, stood at 7,710 members. The *St. Georgs Pfadfinderschaft* originated in Trier in 1929; in 1931 was taken into the JMV; and by 1933, had a membership of 5,891. A scout group, it maintained relations with the International Boy Scouts.

There were a host of other minor, specialized organizations within the JMV. The *Schachbund* (chess league) totaled a surprising 7,712 members. Myriad smaller groups with a combined membership of 60,968 included, among others; drummer corps; orchestral groups; choirs; theatrical groups; pingpong groups; and hobby groups. While the JMV, having inherited this congeries of activities from earlier modes of youth work, remained as a consequence a somewhat amorphous organization, its most dynamic sections (e.g., the *Sturmschar*) had been touched by the new style of youth activity derived from the youth movement.

The general publication for the JMV, *Junge Front,* (after July 1, 1933, renamed *Michael*), became one of the financial mainstays of the central organization. In 1932, its circulation was only 40,000, but, by 1933, had tripled to 120,000; and by 1934, more than doubled again to 245,000.[30] Each age classification also had a publication: *Am Scheideweg* for the *Jungschar, Jungwacht* for the *Jungenschaft,* and *Die Wacht* for the *Jungmannschaft,* with circulations in 1934 of 46,000; 64,000; and 63,000 respectively. The two leadership organs for the JMV were *Jungführer* (circulation 10,000 in 1934) and *Jugendpräses* (circulation 6,000 in 1934). In addition, the larger specialized communities had publications of their own, but their circulations were quite small.

There were several other Catholic organizations for youth not associated with the JMV, and formed for occupational groups. The *Gessellenverein (Kolpingsfamilie)* was a social and religious association for journeymen, founded in 1846 by Adolf Kolping, the "workers' priest." Active members had the right to stay overnight in any of the Kolping Houses located in the larger cities. On special occasions, the members wore uniforms consisting of orange shirts, blue mountaineers' vests, and blue trousers. The *Werkjugend* was the youth organization of the Catholic *Arbeiterverein* of west Germany. There was also an organization for young, clerical personnel, the *Jungkatholischer Kaufmännischer Verein.*

All in all, in 1933, one and one-half million Catholic boys and girls belonged to one or several of the countless Catholic organizations still thriving in Germany. In the spring of 1934 all these organizations incited by the government's first moves against them, became involved in religious demonstrations which the Nazis regarded as protest actions coordinated by the central office in Germany's Catholic Action;[31] and during the winter of 1934-35, these various groups, while keeping their separate identities, tended to unite under their parish priests to form a solid "youth bloc" against the Nazi onslaught.[32]

CHAPTER THREE

Nazi Policy Toward Catholic Church

Hitler's Absolutization of Politics

Apparently, Hitler did not consider a "final solution" in dealing with the churches. On the one hand, his policy suffered from a lack of comprehension of what religion was ultimately about; while on the other, he was all too aware what median ends could be served by an ept manipulation of the "religious" forces in society. As Hans Buchheim points out, what made conflict between Nazism and the churches inevitable and incessant was Hitler's absolution of politics.[1] As evidence of this attitude, Buchheim analyses Hitler's account in *Mein Kampf* of his reactions to the news of the November 1918 revolution in Germany and to Germany's imminent defeat:

> *Now all had been in vain. In vain all the sacrifices and deprivations, in vain the hunger and thirst of endless months, in vain the hours during which, gripped by the fear of death, we nevertheless did our duty, and in vain the death of two million who died thereby. . . .Was it for this that they died, the soldiers of August and September, 1914. . . ? Was that the meaning of the sacrifices which the German mother brought to the Fatherland when in those days, with an aching heart, she let her most beloved boys go away, never to see them again? Was it all for this that now a handful of miserable criminals was allowed to lay hands on the Fatherland?*

> *What now followed were terrible days and even worse nights. Now, I knew that everything was lost. . . .In those nights my hatred rose, the hatred against the originators of this deed.*

> *In the days that followed, I became aware of my own destiny. . . .Kaiser Wilhelm II was the first German emperor who extended his hand to the leaders of Marxism without guessing that scoundrels are without honor. While they were still holding the imperial hand in their own, the other was feeling for the dagger.*

> *With the Jews there is no bargaining, but only the hard either-or.*
>
> *I, however, resolved now to become a politician.*[2]

As Buchheim interprets this passage, Hitler was dealing with a religious question he refused to see as such; in other terms, he failed to confront the existential question of the meaning of suffering and death. Still less did it explicitly occur to him that the slaughter of German soldiers might have had no final meaning. He posed a question, but sought only one answer—one he already recognized and was to find in action—a decision to enter politics and right a great wrong, to avenge himself on the Marxists and the Jews. His politics was one of vivid categories: ally or enemy. There would be "no bargaining, but only the hard either-or."

Thus, Hitler certainly was not practically opposed to religion in the first years of his regime, and indeed appears to have recognized in established faith so much political capital. In an interview on April 26, 1933 with the Catholic Bishop Berning of Osnabruck, Hitler gave all sorts of assurances about the Church's position which turned out to be bald-faced lies. But lies are sometimes revealing, and one dealing with the preservation of the confessional school reveals Hitler's characteristic attitude toward the utility of religion:

> *A black cloud looms over Poland. We need soldiers, believing soldiers. Believing soldiers are the most valuable. They risk all. Therefore we shall retain the confessional schools in order to bring up believers....*[3]

This utilitarian favoring of religion is found even in Martin Bormann, surely one of the most anti-Christian Nazis, as late as 1940. In that year, he came into conflict with Alfred Rosenberg over the latter's attempts to have a new plan for religious instruction drawn up by Reichsbishop Müller, and introduced in the schools. Here, a new National Socialist confronted an old one; for Bormann, Rosenberg's conceptions of German Christianity were probably as irrelevant as those of the traditional churches. In a letter to Rosenberg, he argued that no synthesis between National Socialism and Christianity was possible. But for the time being, Bormann was not prepared to interfere with the traditional form of religious instruction. Such instruction was useful for training in ethical behavior. The Ten Commandments represented "for most of the citizenry. . . .the only remaining guide for ethical conduct and an orderly life in the community." Traditional religious instruction ought not to be done away with until it could be replaced with "something better."[4]

In either case, Hitler needing devout soldiers, or Bormann needing some cement to hold society together, Christianity was a means to an end, but a better means could surely be devised. Eventually, though there was no great hurry, Hitler's form of politics, the "either-or" thinking supported by a racial outlook, would substitute for religion. Finally, that is what the Hitler Youth and the Nazi policies toward the schools were meant to accomplish: to create a new basis of morality.

Hitler's misunderstanding of religion

Hitler's conversion from an attitude of indifference toward religion to outright enmity was made certain by the resistance he encountered when he attempted the *Gleichschaltung* (coordination) of the churches. He apparently assumed that the churches, like the *Reichswehr* or any other institution or organization, could be coordinated to Nazi policies and employed in the service of the state. He saw no reason why the churches could not confine themselves to "spiritual" matters, and leave alone all other questions, which to him were "political." This fact is a clue to the psychopathic nature of his personality. He regarded religion simply as a grandiose fraud about an imaginary afterlife; but he failed to observe that religion affects the decisions of daily life. Having no conscience himself, he did not connect religion with morality. Recognizing no moral limitations on his own destructive behavior, he failed to understand that religion could pose moral limitations on the behavior of others, and he could comprehend opposition from clergymen only in terms of their probable greed, self-interest, or fanaticism, never in terms of an opposition based on a fundamental disagreement about the purpose of man on earth.

Had he realized these basic differences, he might have been much more savage in his dealings with the churches. As it was, Hitler in these early years was not apparently fanatical toward religion. In many ways, he was the complete politician. He never let National

Socialist principles interfere with his political policies and never let minor political affairs interfere with major ones.   Foreign policy was of course paramount, and although he ultimately intended to divest the Catholic Church of its "political" power in Germany, he did not move so quickly in that direction as to jeopardize his international image; thus, Hitler regarded the concordat he concluded with the Vatican in 1933 much more as a great diplomatic stroke than as a regulation of affairs with the Church.   What he did have to say about the Church at that time indicates that he regarded the concordat as a major step in its *Gleichschaltung,* as he put it, obligating the bishops to the state.   His own persistent demand in the negotiations leading to the concordat had been that priests must stay out of politics, which apparently he conceived as a significant step in excluding the Church from public life.   When the Saar plebiscite scheduled for January 1935 loomed on the political horizon, Hitler tried to appear cordial toward the Vatican and continually held open the prospect of further negotiations over matters of dispute, (after all, 70 per cent of the people of the Saar were Catholics).   When the vote in the plebiscite had been counted, Hitler abruptly informed the Vatican he would make no concessions on the matters in dispute.

While in matters concerning youth, Hitler again was at first more politic than fanatic; the conflict here was more critical since long-range political objectives were at stake.   Hitler could tolerate much from the Church, provided he had youth on his side; but as long as youth strayed, the day of attaining his ultimate goals was postponed.[5] Even here, he moved gradually, and only when other means had failed did he smash the Catholic youth organizations, and that was done stepwise by piecemeal suppressions.   Hitler could conceivably have tolerated the existence of Catholic youth organizations provided they had in no way conflicted or competed with the Hitler Youth, but neither Catholic Youth nor the Catholic Church could voluntarily accept such a restriction of what they saw as an essential activity.

The totalistic nature of Nazi thinking

A document from the days of concern over the Saar plebiscite reveals much about the official Nazi attitude toward religion.   It comes from the hand of Germany's Plenipotentiary to the Saar, Bürckel.

On October 17, 1934, Bürckel wrote to Foreign Minister Neurath to suggest how the latter might have the German ambassador at the Vatican bring up the matter of the attitude of the clergy in the Saar. Disturbed by talk that the Church should be neutral in the plebiscite campaign, he maintained the priests of the Saarland as German citizens had no right to be neutral; to the contrary, they were obliged by God's law to speak out for Germany. Bürckel's reasoning was that (1) "The loyalty of man to his national community as part of the order of creation... [is] ordained by God"; (2) The Church accepts the divine order of creation; (3) Should the Church fail to demand loyalty to the national community from the priests of the Saar, it would clearly violate neutrality, since it would be "taking a biased attitude in favor of those who deny the moral and religious importance of the solidarity of the national community... [that is] the opponents of Germany....". If the Papacy prevented its priests from speaking out, it would deprive itself of the protection of the concordat because it had in fact denied its bond with the national community and could therefore enjoy no corporate rights deriving from that national community.

The document had no effect since the ambassador to the Vatican, Diego von Bergen, spared himself the embarrassment of presenting such a thesis by informing the foreign ministry that he had already presented the essential points of Bürckel's note in his own arguments. An argument similar to Bürckel's third point also appears in a.report of June 19, 1934 by the *Sicherheitsdienst* (SD), the intelligence organization of the *Schutz Staffel* (SS). The argument in that report holds that one of the prime purposes of the concordat had been to exclude priests from politics. Priests who nevertheless continued to make unfavorable comments about the new regime and its leading figures had themselves violated the concordat, and were therefore not entitled to its protection.[6] In both instances, it is clear that the Nazi recognized no rights against the state and *Volk* community.

Limitations on totalitarian policy in dealing with the churches

Despite the totalistic modes of thought to which the Nazis had indurated themselves, in practical reality Hitler did not have a free hand in dealing with the Church, and was quite aware of the fact.

The greatest limitation on his policy was in a sense self-imposed: politics came first, and particularly foreign policy. Extremism was not always the best politics, and the best Nazis were not always the best politicians. The most extreme Nazis during the early years of the Third Reich often became liabilities when their immoderation alienated groups and states which Hitler needed to keep friendly, or at least neutral. Public opinion in foreign states was the respected deterrent to the extension of totalitarian power within Germany; if, for example, Hitler was to take advantage of divided opinions in foreign lands, he could not simply proceed with all the force at his disposal to change the churches as he saw fit since what he would then gain in the domestic arena he would lose in international viability. Reichs-bishop Müller's rough and inept handling of the administration of the Evangelical Church, which he was supposed to "coordinate," alienated very influential churchmen in Britain who had been in the habit of supporting German claims for a redress of grievances. In the end, this, as much as the discord he caused at home, led to Müller's falling from favor.[7]

August Jäger, legal administrator of the Reich Church, also lost his post because of overt fanaticism. He made great efforts to enforce Nazi policy against the Evangelical Church, even arresting the Evan-gelical bishops of Würzburg and Bavaria. But he outraged British churchmen and even the Evangelical Church's pro-Nazi German Christian faction, and was forced to resign.

Hans Kerrl, Reich and Prussian minister for ecclesiastical affairs, was a rabid Hitler worshipper. He once wrote that "National So-cialism is itself a religion ... [which] ... not only recognizes, but actually experiences daily its obligations to God and the divine order of things." Kerrl continually urged that Ambassador Bergen be re-placed; but he was not, probably because he was an extraordinarily effective ambassador. In fact, Kerrl's intuition was correct; Bergen was not a Nazi, but an old school diplomat. But his presence at the Vatican was more useful to the Nazi state than that of a convinced Nazi of the caliber of Kerrl or Bürckel.

The relative caution which Hitler exercised in his policies toward the Evangelical Church was even greater in his dealings with the

Catholic Church. Hitler did not wish to provoke a public denunciation by the Pope, which would have had worldwide and continuing repercussions; nor did he wish to alienate the loyalties of the German Catholic population by taking direct action against their bishops.

There were also serious limitations imposed upon Nazi policies. At the head of the Church, stood the Papacy, which through its nuncios and through foreign ambassadors resident at the Vatican, maintained diplomatic relations with most of the major powers and, anachronistically, with the Bavarian state government until May 31, 1934. Also, the Catholic Church within Germany itself at the various levels and centers of power was a formidable opponent. Viewed as a governmental system within the administrative structure of the Catholic Church, it was the product of an earlier age with no modern parallel. At the top were the archbishops possessing enormous powers and great prestige, occupying positions which had long since ceased to exist in European secular governments; that of provincial governors. Where in modern European administrative systems local officials are agents of the central government, bound thereto by modern lines of communications, the bishop's office is a product of an age in which slow communications made local initiative, and therefore local authority, essential. Brought forward into modern times, the Church's administrative structure was relatively slow moving. But based as it has been on local agents possessing considerable prestige in their own right, this structure has perennially supplied the Church with highly esteemed, gifted, and tested leaders in a position both to succor the faithful and deal with the powerful. Thus, the German prelates were, in general, men capable of standing up to anyone in the Nazi state. Among the Catholic community at least, only Hitler could equal them in stature. No minister of the state, no *Gauleiter,* no party official could be regarded as the social counterpart of a cardinal archbishop, who was veritably a prince of the Church. (Some of the prelates were, moreover, of highly distinguished lineage; Bishop Galen of Münster, for one, could trace his noble ancestors in Westphalia back seven hundred years). Add to all this the Catholic belief that bishops hold their office as spiritual descendants of the Apostles, and one begins to sense the unique authority inherent in the position. In dealing with such personages, direct coercion was impolitic. Only indirect coercive pressures were politically safe.

One of the most important factors in the continued existence of Catholic organizations was the energy and effectiveness of the parish priest. The *Sicherheitsdienst* records contain a number of complaints that local Nazi organizations could make no headway because the local priest had set himself against them. There are even reports attributing reduced membership in National Socialist organizations to pastoral opposition. Although a certain sign of a priest's success was his ability to hold down membership in National Socialist organizations; his removal by the police would by no means solve the problem. Since the Catholics of his parish were truly committed to and reliant on him, his forcible removal could only cause unrest and further alienate the parish.[8]

Another source of constraint on totalitarian power lay in the communications networks, both formal and informal, within the Catholic Church. This was perhaps least efficient at the top. The bishops of Prussia and the Upper Rhenish province met annually at Fulda, site of the grave of St. Boniface. The archbishop of Munich-Freising attended as representative of the Bavarian bishops, who had a regional conference of their own. There was no real central authority within the Church of Germany. Cardinal Bertram, as head of the Fulda Conference, kept up a certain amount of correspondence with the other bishops during the year, but that was limited in scope. What was effective about the Fulda Conference was the prestige accorded to the letters issued after its annual meetings. The pronouncements were awaited with anticipation and read from every pulpit in the land on the same Sunday. Condemnations of Nazi doctrines and policies which came from this source had great weight.

What remained after the Nazis had brought the extensive Catholic press under control was a communications network which was very primitive, and, because of its primitiveness, very durable. Viewed solely as such, the Church hierarchy's contacts with the people looked generally like this: on Sunday morning, Catholics were spiritually obligated to report to central meeting places to receive messages delivered orally by persons who played important parts in many of their lives, and whom they were likely to know personally. The police had great difficulty controlling this sort of communication. They could take action against a priest after he had spoken, but the primitive spoken word could not be censored before it was spoken. The future remarks of a priest could be controlled by imprisoning him; but that in turn might be denounced by his bishop, who could not be arrested without bringing the state deeper into a repressive policy than it was willing to go. Subtler restrictive measures had to be found if possible, and were. On the other hand, the pronouncements of bishops could be restrained, if need be, by taking action against the lower clergy, as came to be the case with Cardinal Faulhaber, cardinal archbishop of Munich-Freising,[9] and with Bishop Count Clemens August von Galen, bishop of Münster.[10]

An example of the devices and avenues of communications between Catholic clergy, and from the clergy to the laity is provided by police records from Essen of the transmission, by Catholics, of a violently anti-clerical poem which originated in Speyer where thousands of copies had been distributed, presumably by Nazis. The poem found its way to Essen in the June 20, 1934 issue of a clandestine nationwide publication for priests, the weekly *Katholische Korrespondez* (Münster). The teachers of Catholic School No. 7 in Essen received the paper, and there, a police informant copied the poem. On Sunday, a priest read the poem from the pulpit of the Cathedral remarking only that here was a document of the times which spoke for itself, a comment which was intended as an implied criticism of the regime. A day or so later, a priest in Catholic School No. 1 read the poem to his students and wrote it on the board, and a police informant recorded the fact.[11] Three channels were employed in the transmission of this poem: a clandestine publication, the pulpit, and a classroom. To close effectively all those avenues would have involved the police in a variety of intrusions into sensitive areas, and constant vigilance by informants and repression by police authorities. That was a formidable task never completely accomplished by the Nazis.

One great benefit of the flow of information within the Church, and its organizations, was its efficacy against official lies. In June 1934, for example, Nazis tried to implicate a Catholic youth in a murder. The charge was effectively refuted through communications within the JMV, and in at least one instance, from the pulpit. What otherwise might have been a disturbing charge was dispelled by information. The murderer was, in fact, a member of the SA.[12]

The inevitability of conflict

Conflict between the Catholic Church and the Nazi state was inevitable. Church - sponsored organizations and religious values blocked the expansion of Nazi organizations and Nazi ideology. In examining the conflict in the ideological realm, we may turn to the extreme situation of the concentration camp. How could the Nazi system develop a good SS man if he were plagued by a Christian conscience? A different sort of ethic was needed. The process of supplying one was not entirely successful, and gentle feelings which subverted the SS ideal had simply to be repressed. Bruno Bettelheim observed in the concentration camp that a nonsadistic SS could be at least as dangerous as a sadistic one. If a prisoner being beaten by an SS appealed to his mercy, the sadistic SS enjoyed the beating all the more because the prisoner's humiliation further gratified his sadism. But an appeal to the mercy of an SS who was a nonsadist, and apparently most of them were not sadists, was more serious, since this SS man had to repress feelings of mercy or sympathy which threatened his image of what an SS ought to be. This internal threat to his identity was presented externally in the form of the begging victim. Enraged by the threat to his self-image, the SS man could vent that rage on the victim.[13]

The larger point to be made from this example is that the compassion taught by Christianity, and the savagery taught by Nazism were simply not compatible; not within the same individual, and not within the same state. The values of one or the other ultimately had to be suppressed or repressed. Nazism was an inversion of Christianity, a devil's mass with Christian values turned upside down. In place of love was hate; in place of humility, racial pride; in place of gentleness, brutality.

Tension in the ideological realm was compounded by the existence of overlapping areas of activity. The fabric of the Catholic Church was deeply interwoven with that of society and state in Germany. While this was a source of permanence for the Church, and set limits to totalitarian incursions, it was also the source of constant vulnerability, and of a thousand frictions with Nazism. Had church and state been as separate as in France, there would have been fewer occasions for conflict; or, had Catholics been apathetic and inactive, had Catholic organizations been narrow, weak, and without vitality—separate from, rather than engaged in the vital functions of society —state and Church might have coexisted more or less peacefully, despite their vast basic differences. But the points of irreconcilability were constantly bared as the expanding totalitarianism pressed into areas already occupied by the Church. The most crucial of these areas of confrontation was that occupied by the rising generation. The questions of religious education in the schools, and the role of Catholic youth organizations could not be resolved to the satisfaction of both parties; for here the world-views of each were set into explicit and general confiict, here would be formed the ideal and conscience on which their respective futures rested.

Nazi advantages in the struggle

Some of the specific powers enjoyed by the Nazi state in its action against Catholic associations play a large part in this narrative. But in addition to the array of physical, economic, and juridical powers which the Nazi regime could invoke, a few more general advantages should be mentioned here.

One of the chief advantages was Nazism's ability to make use of traditional values. Chief among these were patriotism, a strong sense of duty to the state, and finally, the German sense of legalistic formalism.

That Hitler was the duly constituted head of the German government most Germans would not have doubted. That he was advancing German nationalistic aspirations was no less certain. Nazism played upon the Catholic conscience. Catholics had dual loyalites: they wanted to be loyal to Germany on the one hand, and to the Church and Christianity on the other. Most of all, they wanted to believe that in being loyal to one they were also being loyal to the other. Nazism joined the symbols of national loyalty to the regime and tried to make all who had any other loyalties which were not subsumed under their loyalty to the state feel that they were not loyal Germans. To the degree that they were successful, opposition to the regime seemed like treason to the Fatherland.

This tactic was often employed by the Nazis, probably because they really believed what they said. As a Hitler Youth appeal put it:

. . . The German Youth has placed its honor before the judgment of history. . .as creators and bearers of the unity of the Third Reich. Do you, Catholic Youth, holding stubbornly to your factional standpoint, want to be branded by the judgment of history as the destructive force which tried to sabotage the unity of the Reich and the shaping of its future? . . . . .

Catholic Youth! The German Volk awaits your historical step, it awaits your act![14]

The Catholic youth preferred to believe that through supporting their own organizations, they were doing what was best for the Reich —preserving its Christian basis.

In a study of certain Catholic diocesan newspapers in the period before the Second World War, the American sociologist Gordon Zahn has observed a defensive reaction to Nazi accusations that Catholics were poor patriots. The reaction the diocesan press took was to emphasize the great sacrifices made by Catholics in previous wars, a reaction which by "a tragic irony . . . probably contributed to the total consensus demanded by the political community."[15] The power exercised here was not so much the power to create guilt, as the power of "shaming", of subjecting to public disapproval. It is an extraordinarily effective power; for the power to shame is the power to humiliate and to isolate, for no bystander wants to share the humiliation of the victim.

The German Catholic bishops were by no means immune to the appeal of patriotism and nationalism. A striking example concerns the Saar. Ecclesiastically, the Saarland remained under the bishops of Trier and Speyer, although politically the region had been placed by the Treaty of Versailles under French administration. Whether this administration should continue, or the Saar should return to Germany was to be decided by plebiscite in 1935. In the Saar question, the bishops of Trier and Speyer put nationalism above obedience to potential disagreeable administrative orders of the Papacy. To limit the influence of the unconcealed pro-German agitation from the pulpit in the Saar, at one time, the Papacy considered sending an Apostolic Administrator to assume temporarily the powers of the two bishops of the area. The bishop of Trier later assured the German government that had that happened, both he and the bishop of Speyer would have resigned.[16]

Another asset to Nazi totalitarianism was the German emphasis on formal legality. This would appear to be the very bulwark of a free society, but it had its other side. To be acceptable, an action had to be legal; this *could* mean, in practice, that as long as a thing was legal, was in good order, and issued from proper authorities, it was also acceptable. One's duty toward the law was clear; and particularly when so much was at stake, one did not need to inquire about the spirit behind the law. I suspect that as time went on, this mentality became a refuge. Even if a law were profoundly immoral, provided that it was done up according to form, and one's duties toward the law were clearly defined, the clearest course of action was to execute and to obey the law. This mentality was very important to the regime because there were simply not enough Nazi fanatics to staff all of the administrative and police offices of the German Reich.

Another general advantage of Nazism was the division of the opposition. The Nazi regime was rarely opposed by a solid front on any issue of vital importance to it. During the early years of the regime, there were a few bishops within the Catholic hierarchy who looked with favor on the work of "national reconstruction". The Catholic aristocrat von Papen, who was in contact with some of those bishops, did great service for the regime in negotiating a concordat with the Vatican. On the domestic front, he created and supported a Nazi front organization, the *Arbeitsgemeinschaft Katholischer Deutscher,* until it was pushed aside by the Nazis themselves. After Austrian Nazis murdered Chancellor Dollfuss, Hitler sent Papen as German minister to that Catholic country, where he was soon using his excellent Catholic connections to spy on the correspondence between the nuncio at Vienna and the Vatican.[17]

A final advantage enjoyed by the Nazis in pursuing their programs was some of those programs, such as that for the interdenominational, or secular school, had behind them trends which had nothing to do with Nazism. The *Gemeinschaftschule* had been advocated by socialists, liberals, and professional teachers' organizations, and under the Weimar constitution had been envisaged as the norm.[18]

The marshalling of national symbols; the existence of potential collaborators; the lack of a united opposition; and the adoption of secularizing programs which struck a responsive chord in some segments of German society made it possible for the Nazi regime to proceed in a piecemeal fashion; to execute its policies first in those areas, or with those persons, or with those programs, where there was the greatest possibility of success.

CHAPTER FOUR

Catholic Youth and the Concordat

*The Catholic Church and National Socialism:
ideological and political conflict*

Hitler had sound historical reasons for wanting to exclude priests from politics. From 1930, the Church in Germany had increasingly opposed National Socialism.

The initial Catholic denunciation may have resulted from a Nazi political maneuver. On March 29, 1930, the Center party's Brüning became chancellor in a cabinet which included the parties from the Center over to the nationalist parties on the right, but no Social Democrats. The Nazi battle cry, that it fought world Jewry and Marxism, was temporarily without a direct political object of attack. Some Nazis adapted to the situation by attacking the Center party as a blasphemy upon religion, and a betrayal of Christianity to atheistic Marxism. If the Center was misusing religion for political goals, the Nazis would demonstrate that they were the true Christians. Party members, sometimes in closed formation bearing flags, began attending church in uniform.[1]

It may have been some such demonstration that caused a pastor in Kirschhausen to announce that Catholics were forbidden to belong to the Hitler party, that as long as a Catholic remained a member of the party, he was to be denied the sacraments, and that members of the party were not to be permitted to attend burials or other religious events as a corporate group. The *Gau* leadership of Hesse took the matter up with the episcopal chancellery of Mainz. On September 20, 1930, the chancellery replied that the pastor's statement had been the result of his inquiry to the chancellery office as to what position he should take toward the NSDAP. The chancellery went on to condemn beliefs of National Socialism, as embodied in its statement concerning "positive Christianity" in Article 24 of the party program, pointing out that a Catholic could not adhere to that statement without denying important points of his faith.[2]

Nazi doctrines attracted other denunciations as the party grew in size. In February 1931, the eight Bavarian bishops condemned the party's racism, rejection of the Old Testament, denial of the primacy of the Pope, establishment of the moral feeling of the German race as a standard of morality, and plans for an undogmatic German church. The matter of admission to the sacraments the bishops left to the individual priest, who was to distinguish between the active propagandist and the simple member who had been drawn in. On March 5, 1931, the bishops of the Cologne church province issued another condemnation, and in August 1932, the annual Fulda conference issued a declaration against the errors of National Socialism.

Open political conflict between the Church and Nazism began on April 11, 1932, when the bishops of Prussia urged their flocks to elect to the Prussian Landtag deputies who stood for the protection of confessional schools, the Christian religion, and the Catholic Church. On July 12, 1932, those bishops issued a pastoral letter of similar content concerning the Reichstag elections. During February 1933, the Fulda conference urged the faithful to vote for the same sort of deputies. Although the bishops did not mention the National Socialist party by name, obviously they were not recommending Nazis.

Apparently the Church's stand did help sustain the Center party, and deny voters to the Nazis. Between 1928 and the last free election in 1932, the Nazi vote rose from 2.6 per cent of the total, to an astounding 37.3 per cent in the first election of 1932; dropping to 33.1 per cent in the second. Only the other extremist party, the Communists, made substantial gains during this period. Yet through all this, the Center Party held steady, and even grew slightly in its proportion of the vote. Meanwhile, the middle class parties lost eighty per cent of their votes dropping from a quarter to less than three per cent of the total vote, and collapsed as a political force. Even the conservatives, who did much better, lost forty per cent of their previous proportion of the vote.[3]

Despite the success of the Church in protecting the Center party, by the time the Fulda Conference opened in February 1933, the position of Nazism was secure. The size of the Nazi vote, by far the largest of any party, made it increasingly difficult to deny the NSDAP's clamor for power; with Germany in economic crisis and on the brink of civil war, Hitler and his now vast contingents of armed SA seemingly had the power to precipitate or prevent that catastrophe. Generals influential in the army looked with favor upon a Hitler government, and Franz von Papen, who had had his turn at governing in an impossible situation and who had gained great influence over President von Hindenburg, persuaded the latter to accept Hitler. The old general appointed Hitler as chancellor on January 30, 1933. Papen was appointed vice chancellor, supposedly to keep Hitler in check.

Hitler immediately called for new elections in March. On February 27, the Reichstag building was engulfed by fire, and the Nazis raucously accused the Communists of arson and terrorism. On February 28, Hitler persuaded Hindenburg to use his presidential powers to issue a Decree for the Protection of People and State which suspended civil liberties. This laid the foundation of the totalitarian regime, and most police orders issued thereafter cited in their headings this decree as the source of their legality.

The elections, held on March 5, 1933 in an atmosphere of terror and hysteria, improved still further the position of the NSDAP. When religious services were held at Potsdam to celebrate the first meeting of the newly elected Reichstag, Hitler and Goebbels, nominal Catholics, took the opportunity publicly to rebuff the bishops for interference in politics. During the church services, Hitler and Goebbels were away laying wreaths on the graves of fallen storm troopers, with attendant publicity.

On March 23, as a result of discussions with Monsignor Kaas,[4] leader of the Center party, Hitler proved much more conciliatory in his speech to the new Reichstag.

> *The Government, being resolved to undertake the political and moral purification of our public life, is creating and securing the conditions necessary for a really profound revival of religious life. . . . The National Government regards the two Christian Confessions as their weightiest factors for the maintenance of our nationality. They will respect agreements concluded between them and the federal states. . . . The National Government will allow, and secure to the Christian Confessions the influence which is their due, both in the school*

and in education. . . . The Government of the Reich, who regards Christianity as the unshakable foundation of the morals and moral code of the nation, attaches the greatest value to friendly relations with the Holy See and is endeavoring to develop them.[5]

Thus, Hitler seemed to recognize the churches as the foundation of the new order, guaranteed their rights, guaranteed the existing concordats with the states, and promised to secure the influence of the churches in the schools.

Churchmen were somewhat relieved by this statement,[5] and if soon it no longer seemed auspicious, it did make it possible for them later to protest Nazi policies on the grounds that they were not in accord with the expressed wishes of the Führer. Veiled threats that the government would not permit "the commission with impunity, or the toleration of crimes," interlarded between the guarantees, passed unnoticed.

Following Hitler's speech, the Center party, the support of which was needed for the requisite two-thirds majority, joined in voting for the Enabling Act which gave the existing cabinet full powers to rule by decree.

Hitler with full powers

The German bishops dealing with a party with the full power of the state at its disposal, a party whose leader was now the legitimate head of the government, quickly modified their earlier stand. The episcopate did not change its attitude toward the errors of National Socialism, but the Fulda Conference now declared that in view of the assurances of the chancellor its "general prohibitions and warnings" were no longer necessary.[7] What this meant in practice was indicated by Cardinal Bertram's new instructions for the pastoral care of party members: Nazis were to be allowed to receive the sacraments and could be admitted to services in uniforms, though the appearance of political demonstrations should be avoided.

A few churchmen were relieved. Bishop Burger, auxiliary bishop of Freiburg, welcomed the wave of "national renewal" and asserted that the "goals of the Reich government had long been the goals of the

Catholic Church." His archbishop, Conrad Gröber, instructed his clergy to "assent affirmatively" to the regime and steadfastly to co-operate with it.[8] Despite the decisive vote of the Center party for the Enabling Act, and the relaxation of proscriptions by the bishops, conditions did not go well for Catholic officials in the new Germany; and within two weeks of that relaxation, Cardinal Bertram was protesting to President Hindenburg the wholesale dismissal of Catholic civil servants in eastern Silesia. On April 14, 1933, the cardinal archbishop of Cologne, the archbishop of Paderborn, and the bishop of Osnabrück joined in a declaration, noting with the deepest concern that these days of national revolution were for many loyal officials days of suffering. The next day, the bishops of the upper Rhenish church province joined in a similar protest.

Hitler undertook to conciliate the bishops without, in effect, conceding anything. On April 26, he reassured a conference of diocesan representatives in Berlin that he had no intentions of waging a *Kulturkampf,* or of interfering with the rights of the Church. He would never allow secular schools to replace confessional ones. Catholic associations were in no danger if they supported the state and promoted Christian and community spirit. Officials were being dismissed for reasons of economy, and in order to make room for National Socialists, but there were sure to be posts left over for the Center party. Two days after this interview. Hitler sent a single answer to an accumulation of letters from Cardinal Bertram. Although he reminded the cardinal of the disabilities Nazis had suffered under Center party rule, he assured him that he would not remove any official from public service because of his religion, nor would he act against Catholic associations if they were not hostile to the regime.

The concordat

Hitler soon matched his conciliatory words with gestures toward the Vatican. Toward the end of March, the Vatican secretary of state, Cardinal Eugenio Pacelli, seems to have discussed the question of a concordat with Msgr. Kaas, who was then in Rome. On April 2, Kaas had an interview with Hitler,[9] If a concordat was discussed, Hitler had reason to be willing, for the conclusion of a treaty with the head of the Catholic Church would enhance the international prestige of his regime at a time when it was badly needed and would enable German Catholics to support the regime with fewer reservations. The Vatican also anticipated benefits from an agreement. Since negotiations for a concordat, carried out intermittently from 1919, had always failed because the German government could not at the same time meet the demands of the Vatican, and still get the concordat approved by the Reichstag (which in any case was hostile to the whole idea), the Holy See had instead settled for concordats with the states of Bavaria (1924), Prussia (1929), and Baden (1932). However, the change of the Reich government in Germany radically altered the situation, and the rights of the Church could now receive adequate protection only from an agreement with the central government. After preliminary contacts in Rome through Papen, Kaas, and Goering, Papen, now vice chancellor and a prominent Catholic, was charged with negotiating for the German government. From the very first, probably on Hitler's insistence, Papen intended to make sure that any agreement arrived at removed the clergy from political parties. In Rome, in May, he began discussing with Cardinal Secretary of State Pacelli the question of a concordat. Monsignor Kaas, who had left the Center party to flounder and departed from Germany on April 7, was now resident at the Vatican as an advisor on German affairs. He also took part in the conversations and continued negotiations on Papen's behalf after the vice-chancellor's return to Germany, thus serving something of a dual role. The monsignor provided Papen with a draft concordat which he, Kaas, had helped to prepare in the early twenties. In mid-May, Papen wrote to Kaas his suggestions for changing one article (the later Article 23), since Hitler wanted a clear exclusion of priests from politics. Papen proposed that in this article the Holy See forbid priests to accept any official function in political organizations. That provision, he assured Kaas, was the *sine qua non* for Germany's signing the agreement. The Vatican had difficulty accepting that, and discussions concerning that question continued without resulting in a mutually acceptable formula for the article.

The Holy See decided before going any farther to sound the opinions of the German bishops, and on May 30, 1933, the Fulda conference assembled, joined for the first time in decades by the Bavarian bishops as well. The Vatican sent the bishops a provisional text of the concordat and informed them of the progress of negotiations. There were some sharp contrasts of view among the bishops. Cardinal Schulte impulsively wished the Catholic Church to refuse to deal with the "revolutionary regime." Bishop Preysing of Eichstätt wished the Fulda pastoral to prepare the Catholic people for the "apparently approaching conflict."[10] But the moderate views of Archbishop Gröber, fresh from the negotiations at the Vatican, prevailed. He argued that enmity between church and state would be fatal to both.

The resulting Fulda pastoral, drawn up on June 3, 1933, attempted to render unto Caesar the things that were Caesar's, but also spoke in defense of the Church. The bishops expressed their loyalty to the state, but also demanded their rights. Their demands for freedom to continue confessional schools and confessional teacher training, to maintain youth organizations; to possess a Catholic press; and to continue Catholic charity, they said, did not imply any mental reservation toward the state, but so much had happened during recent months which, from a Catholic standpoint, seemed incomprehensible, that they hoped those events would prove part of a process of fermentation soon to end.

They had much to say about youth. Already, on May 31, the Fulda conference had considered the question of youth organizations, (a question which was soon to replace the dispute over the exclusion of priests from politics as the chief area of conflict), and had addressed a special letter to it. The Catholic youth organizations were in danger. On May 2 - 3, the *Generalpräsidium*[11] and the *Reichsvorstand*[12] of the JMV had met at *Haus Altenberg,*[13] and registered their concern about the dangers to the work of the JMV. Hitler Youth propaganda bombarded the members, the school filled up their free time, officials put pressure upon teachers who assisted the JMV, employers put pressure on employees who belonged or assisted, public agencies reduced their financial aid to the organization, and there was interference with the free use of youth homes and playing fields. The JMV kept the bishops informed of the situation through a commission for youth questions established by the order of the episcopate.

On May 31, the hierarchy therefore drew up a letter to the youth organizations assuring them of the concern and support of the bishops. The bishops rejected the notion that all youth ought to be assembled and educated exclusively by the state.   Rather, the Church demanded full corporate rights for its youth organizations and for their members, and full educational rights for them in physical, spiritual, and occupational training.   Since the state leadership had assented to the freedom of the organizations, and the fulfilling of their special tasks, the bishops expected that the youth organizations would be allowed freedom of activity, and that an indirect destruction of those organizations by irresponsible offices would be prevented.   They found intolerable the insecure position of the youth organizations in the eyes of the law; the prejudicial treatment received by their members in school and work; and the general relegation of members to second class citizenship in those realms, and through strictures on wearing insignia and marching on the streets; and above all, the bishops decried direct or indirect moral pressure placed upon members at school or work.   The property of the youth organizations, also, ought to be guaranteed by the state.   The fact that public aid had sometimes been advanced for the construction of youth homes or playing fields did not invalidate the rights of those organizations to hold property.   In the schools, Catholic youth organizations ought to have the same rights as any other youth organization, and a one-sided official recruiting for a single youth organization ought to be abjured. Appealing to the individual members, the bishops charged the young people to be loyal to their leaders, and work for their groups in a spirit of willing self-sacrifice.

The official Fulda pastoral of June 3 also had much to say about youth. Some of its comments concerning the confessional school were equally applicable to the youth organizations:

> *It is not sufficient that the Church be free only inside of the church, that is, the church building, and in the dispensation of sacraments.   For it lies in its task to permeate the whole life of the man, private and public, and to impregnate it with its own life source.* ...

The pastoral letter also dealt specifically with the youth organizations as such.

> *Far from separating the youth from the whole of the Volk. . . , they wish to be practical schools of Christian character, and, to employ the words of St. Paul, be "race courses" for the training*

*of moral men, and thereby create the prerequisites for valuable
citizenship. Whoever condemns the existence of these youth
organizations in their manifold forms serves the state badly, for
he disdains the religious powers which can be replaced by no
others. If one objects that at least sports for the young have
nothing to do with religion and church, then he fails to understand
that Christianity and Church influence the whole life of the man
and endow physical education with a quite different character
than the purely natural sense of the thing. . . .*[14]

Little more than a week following the Fulda conference, the
Munich Nazis displayed clearly their attitude toward uniformed extra-
churchly organizations on the occasion of a national conference of
the *Gesellenverein.* SA, SS, and HJ assaulted the delegates in the
streets, beating them, and ripping off their orange shirts. The Munich
police, under Heinrich Himmler, looked the other way. On Trinity
Sunday, June 11, the third day of such assaults, two thousand storm
troops assembled near the place where Cardinal Faulhaber was to
celebrate high Mass for the congress. When the cardinal was unable
to obtain any assurances of police protection for persons coming to,
or leaving the mass, he called off the entire congress. The storm
troops then made a victory march through the city before resuming
their man hunt. On June 13, the Bavaria political police forbade
public appearance of Catholic organizations.[15] That same day, storm
troopers hunted down and beat to unconsciousness an important member of the Bavarian People's party.[16]

Meanwhile, diplomacy continued. Cardinal Faulhaber informed
Papen that the Fulda conference took a different view than the government on the question of excluding priests from politics, but did not
wish negotiations to break down because of that fact. Hitler made
it clear that he wanted the clergy excluded from all political activity,
and not merely from the holding of offices in political parties as
Papen had earlier proposed. Besides wanting to forestall Cardinal
Bertram, whom the Vatican wished to take direct part and who had
always proved difficult in negotiations, the vice-chancellor felt that
he would have to negotiate that matter in person, and obtained Hitler's
consent to return to Rome.

The Nazis did not wait for the conclusion of any agreement to begin writing into reality their conception of excluding priests from politics. From June 20 to 23, many Catholic priests active in the Center party, or its Bavarian counterpart, the People's party, were arrested. On June 21, the political police of Bavaria searched houses, and offices of officials of the Bavarian People's party. On that same day, Labor Front leader Dr. Robert Ley made known his understanding of the sphere of church and state when he announced that the salvation of souls did not require Catholic gymnasiums, or denominational workers' associations. Three days later, he branded such associations enemies of the state, and observed that it was high time they disappeared. From Berlin, Erich Klausner, the leader of Catholic Action, and from Breslau, Cardinal Bertram, who served as president of the Federation of Catholic Workers' Associations, protested that latter statement. Cardinal Bertram's stature as head of the Fulda conference, as well as the important part he was likely to play in negotiating the concordat, may have been reflected in the fact that Ley at once declared that he had not really meant what he had said.[17] Nazis nevertheless occupied the offices of, and dissolved the Congress of Christian Trade Unions on June 24. Ley's retraction proved unnecessary in any case, since the illness of an auxiliary bishop prevented Bertram from proceeding to Rome.

On June 26, the deputies of the Bavarian People's party were served with summonses, and all of the party leaders were arrested. Throughout the Bavarian Palatinate, numerous priests who had been active politically were arrested, and many were assaulted in the streets. Speaking at Stuttgart, on June 26, Propaganda Minister Goebbels advised the Center to close up shop, since it no longer had any right to exist.[18] On July 5, in a letter to the Bavaran council of ministers, Cardinal Faulhaber protested that nearly a hundred priests had been arrested in the previous few weeks.

On July 1, the Prussian minister of the interior ordered the Gestapo to occupy the *Jugendhaus* in Dusseldorf, (the headquarters of the *Jungmännerverband*). The alleged purpose was to investigate possible conspiratorial connections with the Center party, and the *Volksverein für das Katholische Deutschland*, (a politically active parent organization for various Catholic occupational associations), and to prevent a removal of capital abroad. The Gestapo announced over the radio that it had closed the offices, and taken into its custody the goods of the youth organization on the grounds that it was an auxiliary of the Center party. Throughout the Reich, local state police took action on their level. The occupation of the offices in Berlin was quite orderly, but in the provinces the fanaticism of local Nazis resulted in many transgressions and illegalities. In all probability as a result of the negotiations at the Vatican, on July 7, two days after the Center party had voted its own dissolution, and one day before the initialing of the concordat, the Prussian minister of the interior rescinded the action against the *JMV*, and the rooms of the *Jugendhaus* were made available to their owners. On the local level, however, and especially in southern Germany, many limitations of activity, confiscations of goods, and outright prohibitions were not retracted. Local authorities used a variety of rationalizations to perpetuate the injustices: they had not yet received instructions concerning this particular organization; orders against public appearances by Catholic youth organizations were reimposed locally on the grounds that the appearance of the groups caused unrest in the populace; or local authorities were awaiting instructions as to whether the *Sturmschar* was really a part of the JMV. The *Sturmschar* especially was victimized by local prohibitions and limitations on its activities.

On June 20, in his first interview with Pacelli, Papen was angrily confronted with reports about the situation in Germany. He informed Hitler, by letter, and by telephone calls, that the arrests of clergy were making negotiations difficult, and obtained a promise that upon the conclusion of a concordat the chancellor would arrange a full pacification between the government and the Catholic people of Germany. The promise may have had an effect, since on July 2, the Pope approved the concordat. Hitler's reassurances proved worthless, especially in Bavaria, where the chief of the political police, Heinrich Himmler, was the real local potentate. The persecution of the Bavarian People's party intensified there, and arrests extended from deputies to members.

On July 3, 1933, at the Vatican, Papen discussed the dissolution of the Center party with Monsignor Kaas and Archbishop Gröber, who had been selected to represent the bishops and was *persona grata* to both Papen and Cardinal Pacelli.[19] Papen found that the Vatican considered dissolution inevitable, and approved, provided that Hitler made an early statement that by that action, peace in Germany would be restored. Dissolution took place before such a declaration. Already demoralized, and under severe Nazi pressure, on July 4, the Bavarian People's party, and on July 5, the Center party dissolved themselves.

The Reich ministry of the interior's department of church affairs had been learning of developments in the negotiations after the event. Now the department director, Dr. Rudolf Buttmann, a long time member of the Nazi party, obtained Hitler's permission to fly to Rome, and negotiate about some of the provisions and wording of the concordat.[20] He spent July 6, 7, and 8 there. The actions of party fanatics in Munich endangered the negotiations in Rome. At the opening session, Buttmann met with Cardinal Pacelli, Papen, Kaas, and Archbishop Gröber. The cardinal secretary of state let fly some heated remarks. The Pope, he said, had received very disturbing reports from the German bishops. If, as it was being said, Hitler had insufficient power to enforce a concordat, then why bother to conclude one?[21] Buttmann and Papen attempted to satisfy the objections of the Vatican by a communique worked out with Cardinal Pacelli, to be issued by the Vatican on the occasion of the initialing of the concordat.

With the initialing today of the concordat between the Holy See and the German Reich, His Eminence Cardinal Secretary of State Pacelli, following preliminary explanations by the representative of the German Reich, Vice-Chancellor von Papen, issues the following statement:

1) The Holy See takes notice that the action taken recently against Catholic organizations, measures which are contrary to the concordat, have in part already been reversed and with the initialing, proceeds on its part with the definite assumption, and expectation that measures which are incompatible with Article 31 will be rescinded immediately and not be repeated.

2) The Holy See proceeds further with the assumption that the boundary between the regions of activity of the Catholic organizations and organizations of the state (or fostered by the state) will be established by agreement between the episcopate and the responsible state offices according to the principles of the concordat within one month's time.

3) The Holy See considers itself assured that with the conclusion of the concordat, freedom in the public proclamation and defense of Catholic doctrine and Catholic principles in the customary form will be guaranteed.[22]

To their chagrin, the German negotiators at the Vatican were unable to obtain Hitler's consent to this communique. He would not assent to the statement that the regions of activity for organizations of church and state should be the subject of an agreement between church and state, and he refused to endorse putting a time limit of one month for such an agreement. Neither did he wish to assent to the rights of the Catholic Church to defend its principles. After telephone calls from the German negotiators at the Vatican, Hitler finally agreed to this decree:

The conclusion of the Concordat between the Holy See and the German Government appears to me to give sufficient guarantee that the Roman Catholic citizens of the Reich will from now on put themselves whole-heartedly at the service of the new National Socialist state.

I therefore decree:

1) The dissolution, carried out without directions from the Central Government, of such Catholic organizations as are recognized by the present treaty is to be cancelled immediately.

2) All measures taken against clerical and other leaders of these Catholic organizations are to be annulled. Any repetition of such measures will in future be unlawful and will be punished according to the normal legal procedure.

I am happily convinced that there has come to an end a period in which it appeared that religious and political interests were unfortunately ranged against each other in an insuperable opposition.[23]

Papen handed the decree to Cardinal Secretary of State **Pacelli** on the occassion of the initialing of the concordat.[24] In his statement to a group of German newspapermen in Rome, Papen expanded the note of optimism in the last paragraph of the decree when he declared that the delimitation of competence between church and state had now precluded the possibility of any conflict.

In Berlin, Hitler was just as optimistic. At a conference of ministers on July 14, he squelched a debate on particular points of the concordat. One should see only the great success, he argued. In the first place, the Holy See had negotiated even though it believed National Socialism to be an enemy of the Church; secondly, the Vatican had entered into good relations with a purely German state and had obligated its bishops to that state, an unreserved recognition of the regime; finally, the Church had withdrawn from activity in political parties and in associations, abandoning, for example, the Christian labor unions.

The Papacy was not so satisfied. It had initialed the concordat, but there were two more steps: to sign and to ratify it. Before proceeding further, the Vatican charged Archbishop Gröber to negotiate at Berlin further clarification of Article 31 of the concordat.[25] Since this article was to serve as a focus of most of the disputes between the Vatican and the Nazi regime for the next several years, it is reproduced here in full.

1. Those Catholic organizations and societies which serve exclusively religious, purely cultural, and charitable purposes, and, as such, are subordinate to the ecclesiastical authorities, will be protected in their establishments and their activity.

2. Those Catholic associations which, in addition to their religious, cultural, and charitable purposes, also serve other purposes, such as social or professional interests, will without prejudice to a possible future inclusion in State associations, enjoy the protection of Article 31, paragraph 1, provided they guarantee to carry on their activity outside any political party.

3. It is reserved to the Government of the Reich and the German Episcopate, to determine by joint agreement which organizations and association come within scope of this article.

4. In so far as the Reich and Länder have in their charge sports and other youth organizations, care will be taken that the members of the same are enabled regularly to perform their church duties on Sundays and holidays, and that they will not be required to do anything irreconcilable with their religious and moral convictions and obligations.[26]

Paragraph four was to serve as a protection against the practice of Hitler Youth leaders of holding interdenominational services, which were forbidden to Catholics, and of scheduling HJ muster early on Sunday morning so that HJ members were unable to attend Mass. Paragraph one referred to charitable organizations, sodalities, and organizations which would be classified as members of Catholic Action, organizations of laymen under the direction of their bishops, devoted to assisting the clergy in their tasks. Controversy in the coming months was to center around paragraph two, which dealt with occupational and youth organizations. Their rights were guaranteed under the provisions of paragraph one provided they were not connected with a political party. Vague provision was made for "possible future inclusion in State associations." Cardinal Pacelli did not like the wording of this paragraph, but the German negotiators were able to pacify him with paragraph three, which left it to the Reich government and the German bishops to negotiate and agree upon the associations entitled to the protection of the concordat.[27]

On July 18, Archbishop Gröber and representatives of the government reached an agreement. Dr. Buttmann issued a statement which left little to be desired. According to the interpretation his statement put on Article 31, Catholic associations listed in paragraph one of the article were to be allowed to conduct their activities independent of governmental interference. Organizations described in paragraph two might, if they wished, be incorporated in national associations but such incorporation would not deprive them of their uniforms or banners, property or independence under their existing constitutions. Members of such organizations were not to be put at any legal or economic disadvantage. Prior to incorporation the German government presumed that a Catholic organization would obtain the consent of ecclesiastical authorities.[28]

In view of this declaration and its acceptance by the episcopate, on July 20, the Holy See consented to sign the concordat, the second step in bringing it into effect. Later that same day Papen told a group of German newspapermen that the concordat guaranteed beneficial cooperation between church and state.

How differently that cooperation was viewed was at once revealed. On July 23, the Nazi party newspaper *Völkischer Beobachter* announced that the Vatican's concluding an agreement meant that it had recognized the National Socialist state. Priests were now obliged to pledge themselves to that state and to its foundations just like any other German citizen. On July 26 and 28, the *Osservatore Romano* contradicted that interpretation. The Papacy dealt with a state in order to guarantee the rights and freedoms of the Church, the Vatican newspaper pointed out. Negotiation of the concordat was based upon canon law, and did not constitute a recognition of the new regime, much less a recognition of the principles of Nazism. On July 29, the Nazi paper replied that the Reich was ruled by National Socialist aims, and that the conclusion of an agreement with the Reich was, in fact and in law, a recognition of the National Socialist government.

Even before the beginning of the newspaper duel, a deeper and more immediately threatening issue had been raised. On July 25, five days after the concordat had been signed, the German government published a law providing for the compulsory sterilization of individuals who were blind, deaf, deformed, or suffering from mental disorders. Passed by the cabinet on July 14 during the same session that witnessed the approval of the concordat, on the suggestion of Papen the law's promulgation had been delayed until after the July 20 signing of the treaty. The decree conflicted directly with Pius XI's encyclical *Casti Connubii* (Chaste Marriage) which declared that "public magistrates have no direct power over the bodies of their subjects . . . they can never directly harm or tamper with the integrity of the body, either for the reasons of eugenics or for any other reason. . . ." When Papen's newspaper, *Germania,* published an article favoring the law, the Holy See condemned that article and instructed the German episcopate to adhere to the principles of the papal encyclical.[29]

The direct conflict over youth, which was to occupy most of the energies of Church and state from this time forward, had been entered on July 29 when Baldur von Schirach forbade to members of the Nazi youth organizations membership in confessional youth groups. Since membership in the Hitler Youth was already required for many jobs, and for any civil service position, such an order put members of Catholic youth organizations at a distinct disadvantage in the new Germany.

The sterilization law sharpened the lines of ideological conflict, and continued actions against Catholic associations and the Catholic press, and the closing of numerous Catholic elementary schools in Bavaria revealed the trend. To consider such questions the German episcopate met in plenary conference at Fulda, and on September 2, Cardinal Bertram, as head of the conference, wrote to the Holy Father stating why the German hierarchy urged an immediate ratification of the concordat. A delay would give the persons in the government opposing the concessions granted in the concordat an opportunity to change Hitler's mind. Ratification would make it possible to proceed against numerous anti-Catholic actions, failure to ratify would worsen the situation. Cardinal Bertram urged using the occasion to demand a redress of grievances.[30]

The Vatican brought its hesitation to an end. On September 5, Cardinal Pacelli spoke with Klee, the charge d'affaires of the German embassy. At first, the cardinal secretary of state asked that a list of Catholic organizations referred to in paragraph two of Article 31 be prepared, and agreed upon before ratification. Moreover, the German government should acknowledge the right to proclaim, and defend Catholic principles in the press, assure the rights of Catholic organizations to appear in public, and promise that members of such organizations should suffer no discrimination.[31]

Probably from concern for the situation in Germany, on September 7, without having obtained the list of protected associations or the guarantee, the Papacy suddenly lowered its demands to a German declaration that the government would consult with the Vatican on any differences of opinion. The German government readily complied, and on September 10, the Pope ratified the concordat. Following the ratification Cardinal Pacelli went to Rorschach, Switzerland, for a vacation. Buttmann asked to be received by Cardinal Pacelli for consultations about the interpretation of the concordat, but the Pope ordered the request refused, according to Ambassador Bergen, so that he could keep a close watch over any negotiations undertaken with Germany.

CHAPTER FIVE

The Anger of Pius XI

The willingness of Catholic youth to cooperate

Attacks on the Church and its organizations continued, despite the ratification of the concordat. The Bavarian state police prohibition, September 19, on all Catholic organizational activities not "strictly religious" particularly threatened the Catholic youth groups.

The head of the JMV, Monsignor Wolker, was being very sympathetic toward the new regime and even wished to put the Catholic youth organizations under the leadership of the state, while retaining for them their special rights and their special tasks. When on June 17, 1933, Schirach received the title Youth Leader of the German Reich, which was primarily a maneuver to empower him to destroy the *Grossdeutsche Jugendbund* (see p. 18 above), Wolker took the title seriously and published his greetings to the Reich Youth Leader, declaring the readiness of the Catholic youth to cooperate in the great community of German youth while retaining their identity, and spheres of action. In September 1933, despite all the measures taken against the JMV, Wolker was still apparently enthusiastic about the Hitler regime. No state truly corresponded to the ideal of the City of God (*Gottesstaat*), he wrote, not the Wilhelmian state, the Weimar, nor the Italian fascist. "But this can and must be said: the new German state bears something of the idea of the City of God in it, in recognizing Christianity as the foundation of the state."[1]

The same spirit of cooperation and appreciation accounts for the instructions published that same month in *Die Wacht* concerning the bearing of flags, and the form of greeting. Marching columns of the JMV were to bear the flag of the new state along with the flag of the organization; the national flag was to be saluted with the outstretched arm; individual members were to greet one another with the "Heil Hitler," and even wandering groups would greet one another in that manner although they bore no flag. The national anthem and the Horst Wessel song were to be sung with the right arm outstretched.[2]

63

The HJ view of cooperation

The Hitler Youth leadership soon made known its own idea of the way Catholic youth could cooperate. In its view, the Catholic youth members had no right whatever to use the Hitler salute, and could best demonstrate fervor by abandoning their Catholic organizations. The October issue of the Hitler Youth publication *Fanfare* accused the leaders of Catholic youth of refusing to take their place in "the great national front of the new state"; still more ominous was a declaration of a Hitler Youth area leader calling upon German boys and girls to join the Hitler Youth and threatening that those who stood apart would be unable in the future to prove that they were Germans. He was following the lead of Schirach, who, on October 6, saw a danger to the Nazi youth in any expansion of the confessions and found the deepest significance of the Nazi movement in the fact that it set national in the place of confessional conviction. As for himself, Schirach declared, he belonged to no church, but believed in Germany. It is no wonder that in addressing a pilgrimage of the JMV during October, Pius XI expressed deep anxiety for the youth of Germany.

In a speech at Elbing on November 6, Hitler revealed his strategy in the clearest terms:

> *When an opponent declares, "I will not come over to your side, and you will not get me on your side," I calmly say. "Your child belongs to me already. A people lives forever. What are you? You will pass on. Your descendants, however, now stand in the new camp. In a short time they will know nothing else but this new community."*[3]

That Hitler was a heathen he often made clear in private; that National Socialism was meant to supercede the "poison" of Christianity is no less certain; but he was not willing to alarm the world by a wholesale attack upon the Churches and religion as long as they did not interfere with the creation of a cohesive base. Time was on his side. Though domestic confrontation with religion had for the present to be borne, long-range ideological warfare, and the campaign for the capture of German youth could forge ahead without direct conflict with the Vatican. On Novermber 26, 1933, Schirach frankly announced that the Nazi party intended to educate German youth in the cult of race and nation and to dissociate the Catholic youth from Catholic organizations; if this were not enough, in a circular to the Hitler Youth, he proposed the celebration of December 25 in remembrance of the Winter Solstice rather than the birth of Christ.

Catholic Youth hold firm

Schirach's decree of July 29, 1933 forbidding to Hitler Youth membership in confessional organizations was typical of his extreme and brutal approach. The decree certainly posed a crisis for members of Catholic organizations, but it just as surely worked to the ultimate disadvantage of the Hitler Youth. First of all; it clearly defined an "either-or" issue for the Church, and for the young Catholics, who in staying with their organizations did so in full consciousness of the potential consequences of their decision. Thus, Wolker's somber predictions in a report of August 20 to the episcopate proved unduly pessimistic. His contention that the Catholic youth groups could not long survive the current pressure brought to bear upon them underestimated the loyalty and courage of their members. After serious initial losses, the membership leveled off, and by October 17, 1933, Wolker could report to the subordinate leadership that of over 5,000 groups, only a few hundred, mostly new groups with shallow roots, had collapsed. Of a membership of over 400,000, the JMV lost some tens of thousands. Moreover, the youth leaders had reported to him that morale in the groups had never been better.[4]

Secondly, the decree against double membership caused organizational difficulties for the Hitler Youth. As the HJ expanded, it needed an ever increasing number of able subordinate leaders; but leadership talent is never abundant. Catholic youth leaders with experience were already active in the confessional groups, and Schirach's order worked against their joining the HJ. The selective factors were bound to militate against the Hitler Youth: those most likely to leave the Catholic youth, and join the HJ were the opportunists and the faint-hearted; those most courageous and loyal were those most likely to stay in their organizations when they came under attack. The best young people would now be those least likely to enter the Hitler Youth.

During the years to come, its inveterate leadership problems made it seem all the more necessary for the HJ to break up the Catholic youth organizations in order to avail itself of their human resources. For example, following a series of complaints about the quality of HJ leadership, especially in predominantly Catholic regions, in July, 1936, the head of the SD of the *Oberabschnitt-Rhein* ordered an investigation.   Three weeks later he received a report from the agent in Adenau.   The agent found the HJ in a very difficult position in the smaller Catholic parishes, where the Catholic youth was much stronger than the HJ.   As for the leadership, he had investigated in Oberwinter and found that an HJ leader had been jailed for a morals offense; in Niederbreisig, the books were in disorder and were under audit; at Ahrweiler and Neuenahr, the HJ was in good hands.[5]

Negotiations over Article 31

The German bishops were obligated to make *ad limina* visits to the Holy See every five years.   Usually, the visits were spread out over the entire year, but in 1933, bishops converged on Rome almost all at the same time, and their complaints about the situation in Germany aroused a growing anger in the Pontiff, who decided to make a public statement, and ordered his cardinal secretary of state to prepare to lodge a strong diplomatic protest.   No statement by any other leader, authority, or group in the world could more effectively have commanded the attention and commitment of public opinion, and Ambassador Bergen did everything he could to dissuade the Pope. He warned Cardinal Pacelli against the "incalculable consequences" which might result and advised instead negotiations with Buttmann. Pacelli declared himself ready to receive Buttmann at any time, but Bergen then replied that first the threat of protest had to be dropped. Any public remonstrance by the Pope, he warned, was certain to be followed by severe conflicts.

An appeal to world public opinion was the Pope's ultimate weapon, but it was not to be employed lightly.   The Church was not dealing with the government of the *Kulturkampf*: willingness to use force had as yet no proven limits in the new Germany.   It must be remembered that essentially, for the Church, souls were at stake, and that the Pope in his supreme pastoral capacity was constrained not to tax to extreme the consciences of German Catholics, nor to expose them to unprecedented repressive reprisals, (a consideration we cannot afford to neglect when recalling the reticence of the Holy See during the rise of the Third Reich). The threat of protest was sufficient to impel Hitler to dispatch Buttmann to Rome, but it was not sufficient to compel him to make any concessions.

In Germany, Monsignor Wolker was counting heavily upon the successful working out of an agreement on Article 31. On August 20, 1933, he had presented to the episcopate a 38-page report concerning the transgressions of the Hitler Youth, and the Nazi state against the JMV.[6] He was able to report that in the north German dioceses the groups were holding up, and, except for appearing in public in large groups, they were able to carry on most of their activities. It was far worse in Bavaria, the Palatinate, Württemberg, parts of Baden, and Thuringia. Confiscation of goods, prohibitions of assembly, and other actions prevented the carrying on of youth activities and threatened the financial resources of the groups. Wolker estimated that the July 1 decree of the Prussian ministry of the interior ordering the Gestapo to investigate the JMV had resulted in losses to the organization throughout the Reich of approximately 10,000 RM, and had also reduced its income. In some regions of Germany, the JMV suffered heavy losses of membership, and the *Deutsche Jugendkraft* (DJK) was particularly hard hit. On July 11, the leadership of the JMV had to impose a special assessment of thirty pfennigs on the members. Wolker did not believe it would be possible to carry on under existing conditions and looked to negotiations with the government for a solution.[7]

On October 3, 1933, Wolker sent a circular to the *Jungmännerverband, Jungfrauenverband, Gesellenverein, Werkjugend, Jungkatholischer Kaufmännischer Verein,* and *Neudeutschland Bund* reporting on the progress of negotiations on the implementation of Article 31. Bishop Berning had written to Buttmann requesting a conference between Hitler Youth representatives, and a representative of the Catholic youth. Eventually, he hoped to include a representative of the Evangelical youth. Monsignor Wolker meanwhile talked to Counselor Usadel in the Reich ministry of the interior. Wolker reported to Cardinal Bertram about the talks, and the cardinal empowered him to negotiate on behalf of the youth associations. Wolker presented his letter of authorization to Buttmann and asked that a date be fixed for the discussions proposed by Bishop Berning. The date was set for October 10, and Dr. Stange of the Evangelical youth was also invited. A preliminary discussion was held which included Dr. Usadel and Walter Conrad, Buttmann's assistant. There seemed to be considerable agreement on basic principles, but little agreement on practical concrete steps to be taken for the protection of members. The government representatives seemed unwilling to believe that existing legal and police protection of Catholic youth against National Socialist formations was proving insufficient. Then Wolker and Adalbert Probst, head of the DJK, engaged in conversations with representatives of the SA concerning scouting. Some progress appeared to be made in arranging the classification of the DJK as a protected organization.[8]

According to Conrad's account, he and Buttmann were honestly trying to arrive at an agreement. Party authorities were basically opposed to the communique Buttmann had issued on July 18, which practically guaranteed the continued existence of the Catholic youth organizations. Himmler wished to exclude *Neudeutschland,* the DJK, *Kreuzschar,* and the *Sturmschar* from the protection of the concordat. Conrad claims that he and Buttmann wanted to settle the matter once and for all by bringing out an authorized list of Catholic organizations falling under Article 31, and on October 2, sent out such a proposal to the federal representatives in the states *(Reichsstatthalter)* for their observations.[9] Himmler, meanwhile, refused to lift the decree forbidding any activity of Catholic associations in the state of Bavaria. According to Wolker, the Reich ministry of the interior assured him that a list of protected associations would be decided upon within one month, and, when embodied in an implementing order, the prohibition in Bavaria would be lifted. No such implementing order was ever issued.

Conrad's version of these discussions seems plausible. It is hard otherwise to account for the euphoria on the Catholic side, which felt that tangible progress was being made. Conrad argues that Buttmann was an honorable man. This also is quite possible. Cardinal Pacelli seemed to think well of him at least as late as December 1933.[10] Moreover, it would be quite natural that officials of the Reich ministry of interior would wish to enforce some restraints upon fanatical policemen like Himmler, whose precipitate actions they were called upon to explain to Church officials. Otherwise, we must assume that Buttmann was guilty of thorough duplicity in issuing his statement of July 18, 1933.   It is more likely, as Conrad argues, that Hitler had again used a basically honest man for dishonest purposes.   If that interpretation is correct, Buttmann would be neither the first nor the last such person.   Buttmann was quite explicit in some of his statements during the negotiations ("We are bound by the stipulations of the concordat and do not at all think to deviate from it."[11]), and stressed that economic pressure against members of the Catholic youth groups was not in accord with the spirit of the concordat.

The announced results of the October 10 meeting, although general, were very encouraging to the Catholics.   The representative of the Reich ministry stressed the clear intent of the government, according to the stipulations of the concordat, to protect the rights of the recognized groups of their property and their chosen way of life, including the wearing of uniforms and insignia.   The youth organizations of Germany were to exercise equal rights, although the Hitler Youth would have a place of honor within the totality of youth; moreover, the HJ representative even stressed that it was not in the interest of the Hitler Youth to use economic pressures to gain members, and there was some discussion of lifting the ban on double membership.[12]

As Hitler had ordered, on October 19, Buttmann arrived in Rome to continue discussions there.   Before he left on October 28, Cardinal Pacelli had subjected him to some very close questioning.   The cardinal asked, for example, why Hitler, who was a dictator, could not impose his will on his subordinates; Buttmann answered that in concluding the concordat, Hitler had acted against the will of five-sixths of his people and that in enforcing it he had to take into account widespread opposition.   On the occasion of the second interview, on October 25, Buttmann was questioned by Kaas and Archbishop Gröber, who tried to draw him into a discussion over the implementation of individual articles of the concordat, which he evaded by saying that he was there merely to negotiate over misunderstandings in the execution of the concordat, but not over executive orders for its implementation, which was the province of the chancellor and cabinet. When Cardinal Pacelli began to pin him down concerning the executive orders to implement Article 31 and asked him whether his declaraction of July 18 was absolutely binding, Buttmann replied that as a written record of the results of his discussion with Archbishop Gröber, it did not have the force of law; and therefore, he could not guarantee that it would be reproduced verbatim in the orders of implementation; upon which, Cardinal Pacelli exclaimed that the statement had been the prerequisite for the signing of the concordat. Buttmann replied that no such statement had been made at the time, and that it was not a part of the agreement, or of the statement issued at the time of the signing of the concordat.[13]

Tension mounted as the talks went on. To Gröber's statement that he took Buttmann's statement of July 18 to mean it was up to the Catholic organizations to decide whether or not they wished to be included in state organizations, Buttmann replied that it was up to the state to decide. Cardinal Pacelli, who had heard rumors that the Nazis intended to declare the Hitler Youth the state youth organization,[14] sprang to his feet and exclaimed that a state monopoly which would destroy the youth, sport, or other Catholic associations would constitute a breach of the concordat; Buttmann cited the phrase from Article 1 "within the limits of the law that applies to all" as ruling. The cardinal secretary of state countered that it was a breach of international law and that international law took precedence over the law of the Reich. With nothing settled, and much suspicion aroused, on October 28, Buttmann left Rome to report to the Führer.

The November Plebiscite

In Germany, Hitler called for a referendum approving the policies of the Reich. Papen, speaking at Essen on November 2, unhesitatingly called upon his fellow Germans to vote "Yes" because Hitler was leading Germany to unity, as witnessed by his guarantee to the churches of the full freedom of exercise of their spiritual office. Cardinal Bertram urged Catholics to vote "Yes", but pointed out that they need not feel bound to vote for single party election lists. The Bavarian episcopate on November 8, 1933 qualified its endorsement very explicitly:

> *It is not our business in the vote of November 12 to endorse the events and decrees of recent months which have filled us with anxiety and sorrows....Catholics will....declare their fidelity towards their Fatherland, and their full agreement with the large views and vigorous efforts of the Führer to save the*

*German people from the horrors of a new war, and the atrocities
of Bolshevism, to assure public order and to obtain work for the
unemployed. . . .On the other hand, as far as the vote for the
Reichstag . . . we leave that to the individual conscience. . . .*[15]

The Bavarian government forbade publication of this pastoral,
and the Bavarian state police ordered it not read to the faithful. On
the day following the referendum, Bavarian Minister President Siebert
expressed his resentment at the bishops and told them it was time to
end the era of political interference by the churches, and put all the
power of Christian principles at the service of the new regime. Goering
put it more bluntly to an audience in Berlin: Germany must not again
be undermined by the "Red Rats" nor the "Black Moles."[16]

The Saar

During November, Goering also spoke at Essen and at Trier.
His insults to the Catholic Church in those speeches so angered Pius
XI that the Pontiff returned to thoughts of a public pronouncement
which would uphold the dignity of the Church. The presence of
Goering in Trier had been no accident. In accordance with the provisions of the treaty of Versailles, in January 1935, the nearby Saarland
was to decide its future status by a plebiscite. Hitler's concern about
the Saar in November 1933 had begun to influence his tactics; the
Reich was unlikely to secure the propaganda boon of having the Saar
returned to Germany by a large majority vote in the plebiscite if the
Saar's 70 per cent Catholic population grew too alarmed. In view of
the need of temporizing in dealing with the Vatican, Goering in provoking the Church had done precisely the wrong thing.

That Goering and Hitler sometimes followed disparate policies
toward the Church was revealed in late November when the cathedral
chapter of Berlin elected Bishop Bares of Hildesheim bishop of Berlin
and in accordance with the Prussian concordat asked the Prussian
government whether it had objections of a political nature to the cand-
idate. The Prussian government intended to reject Bares, but an
inquiry to Bergen brought a response that such a rejection might cause
difficulties with the Vatican; Hitler had ordered that conflict with the
Holy See be avoided. Goering, who was Prussian minister president,

was irritated, and although Bares was not rejected, neither did the Prussian government move to approve his candidacy.

The anger of Plus XI

Papen, who was working to bring about an agreement between the episcopate and the German government concerning Catholic organizations, soon encountered the Pope's irritation over Goering's speeches. By November 11, convinced that the hierarchy would probably accept the inclusion of the Catholic youth into the Hitler Youth, provided that the young Catholics received adequate religious care by chaplains, Papen had asked Archbishop Gröber to have the episcopate make the proposal on its own initiative.[17] When, however, Archbishop Gröber on November 15 ventured to present Papen's ideas, without identifying their author, to a meeting of group leaders in Freiburg, the proposals elicited intense resentment.[18] The Pope was so incensed by the plan that, at first, he wished the archbishop's letter concerning the proposal returned unanswered. Cardinal Pacelli prevented that, but bluntly refused the offer of the bishops to negotiate with the government,[19] then, to resume direct negotiations himself, he asked Bergen when Buttmann was going to return to Rome. He asked again in the first days of December, by which time he had become irritated by the lack of response from Berlin. As soon as these latter inquiries were read to Hitler, Buttmann was ordered to go to Rome.

Despite this gesture, the totalistic claims of the Hitler Youth were continuing to burgeon under sponsorship of state authorities. On November 30, 1933, the *Oberpräsident* of the Rhine province had issued a decree which holds a place among the classics of Nazi legalistic formalism, a decree which he concealed from the Reich ministry of the interior.[20] According to this document, since no implementing orders had been worked out for Article 31, and since no list of protected associations had been agreed upon, there was no formal agreement concerning its interpretation. Until the matter had been finally settled, it was up to the local administrative office to decide how Article 31 was to be applied in their localities.[21] This decree provided the basis in law for a progressive series of actions against Catholic youth organizations which eventually destroyed them. Within a few months, within the administrative areas of Kassel, Wiesbaden, Hildesheim, and Oberbayern, and in the city of Munich the decree had been employed, with various degrees of severity to limit the activity of Catholic youth organizations to the strictly religious sphere. In some cases, local fanaticism exceeded the intent of the *Oberpräsident* of the Rhine province, and local authorities prohibited all activities of Catholic youth organizations, including participation in processions, or of holding religious retreats.

The local leaders in Schweinfurt, misunderstanding an order of the *Gau* leadership of Würzburg which prohibited the wearing of uniforms, on April 25, 1934, simply dissolved the Catholic youth organizations and confiscated their property. That was going too far, however, and upon protest of the Bavarian bishops to Hitler,[22] the Reich ministry of the interior countermanded the order.[23]

Buttmann arrived at the Vatican on December 18, 1933 for further discussions with Cardinal Pacelli. The cardinal informed him during their first discussion that the Pope was distressed by the situation in Germany, and had decided to bring up the question in his Christmas allocution. Using this lever, the cardinal urged Buttmann to present him with something to appease the Pope before the text of the Christmas allocution had been fixed, and explained that the Vatican wished to be satisfied that the German government would negotiate concerning the interpretation of the concordat; that in case the government changed the constitution of the Reich, in the interim, it would assume the financial obligations stipulated in the *Länder* concordats; that dismissals of clerical teachers would be rescinded; and that theological students would be relieved of SA and labor service. That same day, Hitler made his decision. He refused to reverse the dismissals of clerical teachers, again revealing his unwillingness to compromise on policies limiting the influence of the Church on youth, but he acceded to every other demand. Accordingly, in his Christmas allocution, the Pope avoided reference to Germany other than to voice his disapproval of the sterilization law, as he felt in all conscience he must. But on December 27, he subjected Bergen to a severe lecture. Among his remarks at that time he stressed that "he, the Pope, could not renounce Catholic education or youth, nor would he renounce it, he said, strongly emphasizing each word."[24]

The Papacy expected Buttmann to return for further negotiations in February, and Bergen advised that, in the expected period of relative calm, the foreign ministry prepare a defensive note for transmission to the Holy See. The ambassador believed that the Vatican was planning to publish its protests in a White Book, and at that juncture the German government had accumulated no documents with which to refute the Papacy's charges. Bergen, therefore, recommended a strong note from Berlin both to help neutralize the potential effect of a Vatican White Book and to deter its publication.[25] On January 15, 1934, the first of a series of such notes was forwarded to the Curia.

CHAPTER SIX

Priests vs. Nazis

The Nazi state had enormous power; but, that was not enough, for Nazism was not a simple dictatorship, but a *movement* which intended to involve the whole people; and to direct their energies toward national and racial goals. Anything short of that total involvement of its citizens was intolerable imperfection. Anything that stood in the way of that union of active energies was a block to the self-realization of the *Volk*. Any individual who held back from affirmation to the whole, or worse still, diverted or blocked the affirmative energies of others, was a sinner in the truest sense.

Nazi morality judges the Priest

The *Sicherheitsdienst* (SD) reports on Catholic priests did not limit themselves to the bare facts; they were loaded with indignation. The writers of these reports hated some of the priests, hated them as wrongdoers. "Father So-and-So attacks the Nationalist Socialist regime in an unheard of manner" was a common phrase. "Unheard of" things apparently were heard rather frequently. What the phrase really meant was that such things *ought not* to have been heard, ought never to have been said, that those who said such things were bad, narrow, selfish men who held themselves, and others back from the true surrender to state and *Volk,* which was the true morality.

Points of conflict: rights of church and state

Did Nazi morality mean that the Church had no rights? Certainly not, said the SD. The Church had the right to enjoy an unhindered care of souls. In the field of education, it had exclusive rights to teach religion. It had the right to maintain groups which were devoted to "strictly religious goals," as the concordat provided. But the state had its rights too, and it claimed "the totality of education in its spheres namely those of physical education, and training in occupational, and *Volk* community."[1] As Robert Ley, head of the Labor Front, put it more bluntly, the salvation of souls did not require denominational workers' associations.   Schirach's version was: "What has sport to do with confessions?"

On the other hand, the case for the continued existence of the Catholic youth organizations was put very well by the Jesuit priest Fritz Vorspel in a sermon on March 13, 1934, in the cathedral in Cologne.   This, and his other Lenten sermons were printed up as handbills and given a mass circulation in Germany.

> *Parents, church, and school are especially obligated to the education of the young.   The Church is thankful to the state, which cooperates in the education of youth.   It must not be forgotten, however, that the parents above all have the right of educating youth, and this educating concerns the confessional school (Catholic as Evangelical). . . . Important also for Christian education is the shaping of youth's leisure time.   It has contributed to the upbuilding of Christian men in many blessed years. Youth Homes alone are not enough; rambles and wanderings are also necessary.   The solution of the youth question is today a weighty problem.   The filling up of free time is more important even than the confessional schools.   Because it knows what a great effect leisure time has on youth, the Church holds firmly to its youth outside of school and home.*

Father Vorspel then went on to cite a few of Schirach's poems which he said were not compatible with the Christian spirit.[2]   Implied in these remarks, are the two reasons why the Catholic Church fought so hard to retain its youth organizations: (1) it recognized in the legacy from the youth movement and the gymnastic associations new forms of education which were extremely effective in developing Christian character; and (2) Catholic youth organizations posed an obstacle to the dissemination among Catholic youth of neo-heathen doctrines which permeated the Hitler Youth.

Points of conflict: the role of the priest

Imbedded in the Church's stand on youth organizations, is the conception that religion goes beyond the church doors and must pervade the whole life.   The main argument for the continued existence of its youth organizations was that they provided training for Christian living, not simply catechism. Without the whole human realm to work in, such training could not be effective. Behind these specific claims lay the general claim which has been the basis for all significant contention between church and state since the Middle Ages, that where a question of morality is involved, the Church is also involved.

Since the *Kulturkampf,* the clergy in Germany had been the leaders of the Catholic community, as was evidenced by the prominent positions they occupied in the Center party, and had become accustomed to speaking out on public issues. In October 1933, Pastor Droll, of Kalle near Dortmund, summarized this position:

> *Catholicism must be brought into politics... It won't do that Catholicism, and the effect of the clergy stop at the church door; all politics and public life must be thoroughly leavened by Catholicism. . . .*

In the first year of the Nazi regime, some priests continued to speak out on public issues and personalities, and often suffered for it. In March 1933, Father Klinkhammer, an assistant priest in Essen, charged that Hitler had trod underfoot points four and twenty-four of the party program. Pointing to the uniformed SA and SS who for some unknown reason had appeared in considerable numbers at the afternoon devotion, he remarked that if Hitler did not create bread for the people, they (pointing to the National Socialists) would turn their guns on him. He was arrested for those remarks. Upon his release, he declared to his religion class that he owed his arrest to louts and liars, which led to his rearrest. Father Klinkhammer eventually was sentenced to six months imprisonment for characterizing a speech of Goering's as "rubbish" (*Mist*). Another priest made equally colorful remarks, calling Röhm a homosexual, and Goering a homosexual and dope addict. For that, he was sentenced to sixteen months imprisonment. In January 1934, a priest, alluding to Hitler's Austrian origins, stated that the Church was already national before a caller had dropped in to order it to be. He also said that one should tolerate the Jews, even if the present day wished it otherwise. In a sermon in February 1934, Assistant Priest Leyendecker in Ronheide, attacking a speech by Goebbels, stated he knew that he stood there for the last time, but that another would come in his place and say the same thing; he had held his silence for a year, but could no longer. As he predicted, he was placed under arrest.

Most priests did not launch attacks on the leaders of the regime —Rosenberg seems an exception, but actually his book, *Myth of the Twentieth Century*, was in most cases made the object of the attack. Occasionally, priests involved themselves in serious trouble by taking stands. In January 1934, a priest in Düsseldorf was taken into protective custody for writing and disseminating pacifist pamphlets among Catholic youth. But most frequent were priestly denunciations of Nazi racism or neo-heathen practices. Father Dionysius gained a reputation among the clergy of the archdiocese of Cologne for his outspoken sermons, his colleagues eagerly recommending to newcomers that they go to the Cathedral on Sunday morning to hear a real sermon. On July 22, 1934, Father Dionysius devoted some attention to Rosenberg's *Myth of the Twentieth Century,* remarking that he did not see how anyone could make the statements in it, and that the thing stank.

Points of conflict: invasions of the Church

Direct Nazi incursions into traditionally Catholic spheres of activity, (including the rather rudimentary use of Church property and buildings for Nazi insignia and propaganda), were more likely to incite priests to verbal, and even physical counterattack.

A priest was arrested in December 1933 for taking away from a Hitler Youth member a poster inscribed "Catholic Youth Hear!"; at the time he seized it, the boy was no longer on church grounds. A month later, another priest was arrested for tearing down a Hitler Youth poster from a tree standing in the church plaza; the trees were on church property, but diverse other groups had used them for posting bills in the past. The matter of posters brought a host of priests to the attention of the police in November 1933. On the twelfth of that month, Hitler staged a plebiscite, calling upon the German people to express their approval of the regime and its policies. Roving groups of National Socialists put up posters everywhere, including the church buildings and their outlying walls. This may in some cases have been more or less defensible in that the church square was the center of community activity, but there is no doubt that on many other occasions it was intentional provocation. A good number of priests were de-nounced for tearing the posters down; one who found a swastika flag flying over his church after the plebiscite imputed it to the "stupid youth," and when he came across a closed column of Hitler Youth shouted after them "Rascals!"

Another form of aggressive action against priests was to greet them with the "Heil Hitler," which in fact proved deeply perturbing to many of the ordained, including one who accused an SA man of giving him the "Heil" only to provoke him. This was often all too true. Many priests who objected to the salute tried to find some way to divert it, for instance by replying "Good day", "Grüss Gott", or Praise be Christ"; many forbade its use during religious instruction in the schools. One priest moved to take constructive action by sub-stituting "Praise be to Christ" and having his students write it out ten times as an assignment; others were quite differently inclined, and when *Hitlerjugend* greeted them with the "Heil Hitler," they boxed their ears. Pastor Droll of Kalle, who must have been the most frequently denounced person in his community, registered his reaction on October 8, 1933, when the SA was marching through the streets. When a SA man urged the civilians to "Heil" the swastika flag as it passed, Father Droll's recommendation was "that rascal ought to be hounded out of town."

Priests strike back

The priests were by no means helpless against intrusions into their churches or spheres of activity. When an area was predominantly Catholic, and the priest a fighter, members of the National Socialist youth organizations sometimes found themselves members of a be-leagured minority. Sometime in February 1934, the JMV was dis-solved in Bad Orb, and as was usual in such cases, the priest respon-sible for the youth group took it very badly. He tried to keep his former charges out of the National Socialist organizations, and youths who did join those organizations found themselves mocked openly by their peers. When girls who had joined the BDM were excluded from play at school, it was apparently with the teacher's sanction; indeed, occasionally teachers in class would ask who belonged to the BDM, and the members who stood were then greeted with jeers. The

Catholic youth showed great spirit in its ranks, and the young greeted one another with the call "Loyalty Heil! We hold together." During an HJ recruiting week, a young Catholic in Oberhausen bei Kirm wrote an inscription on a wall: "Loyalty Heil! We are not weather cocks!" He followed it with the PX insignia.

Priests would often strike back through the pulpit, or through their religious instruction hour at the schools. Particularly in heavily Catholic areas, they could exert great moral and social pressure on a person. In the latter part of 1933, a priest giving religious instruction in a school in Westphalia accused a girl before the members of her class of being a coward because, when the great march of the BDM on the "Day of German Girls" passed by the cathedral in Cologne, she had not stepped out of line to go hear mass in the cathedral. Another priest, the one who assigned his students to write "Praise be to God" ten times, used his religious instruction period that day to ask questions: "Are you Christian or heathen? Is Hitler God, or is Jesus Christ?"

In April 1934, the *Jungvolk* and Catholic *Jungschar* of Solingen-Krähenhöhe engaged in a war of posters. According to the police, members of the *Jungschar* started it by smearing their insignia on the JV Youth Home. *Jungvolk* then put up recruit posters on the Catholic Youth Home, and on the bulletin board of the church. The *Jungschar* removed the poster from the church and replaced it with a sign:

> *Youth, there are dirty fellows at work who have left their card on our Home. These methods call to mind a soviet Germany.*

Jungvolk members Bergfeld and Jüngel removed this sign. At his next religious instruction period, Father Richarz, leader of the Catholic youth organizations, ordered the "two louts in this class," Bergfeld and Jüngel, to "get out." When the regular teacher, a Nazi, and finally, the rector of the school interceded and brought the boys back into the class, the priest walked out. The NS Teachers League proceeded to have him excluded from giving religious instruction.

The school was not their province, and priests could quickly end in serious trouble there. In the spring of 1933, a priest who visited a local school found, and removed a swastika which had been placed there by the SS, with the remark that that symbol did not belong in a Catholic school. He was arrested, and juridically punished. In his church, and in his spiritual capacity, the priest was in a far more tenable position, and could from such a base resist the invasions of National Socialism in a variety of ways: by refusing to admit its symbols in the church; by refusing to add his sanction to National Socialist ceremonies in and out of the church; and by refusing to let *Hitlerjugend* serve mass in uniform, or sometimes serve mass at all.

Discrimination against Hitler Youth as altar boys was a common complaint in the files of the police. In 1935, the vicar general's office apparently made the prohibition general for the diocese of Aachen, alleging that the HJ, as members of an extra-churchly group, did not have the "requisite freedom" to serve as acolytes: "What the youth does, he should do wholely." In reprisal, in order to give youth the "requisite freedom," as he ironically put it, on April 11, 1935, Schirach ordered that the names of HJ members who served as acolytes should be provided to the vicar general's office, adding that it was the Church itself which was clearly taking action against the state youth.

The police were occasionally shocked to find SA men participating in Catholic activities, in one case, even assisting the priest in leading Catholic youth on rambles, but shock at such mixture was more often on the other side. Nazis in closed formation frequently brought flags into the church, and priests who remembered the days when that practice had been forbidden found ways to deal with the situation. On October 8, 1933, in Malbergen, the SA came in closed formation to commemorate the war dead. They wished to stand their two flags in the choir where Catholic organizations customarily placed theirs, but the priest told them that their flags would be in the way. On the occasion of the 1933 Harvest Thanksgiving, the pastor in Dremmen asked the color bearer of the local NSDAP to take the flag out because only church flags were allowed in the church, not political ones. On the same occasion, at a church in the Trier area, a priest ordered the NS Womens' Association to take their flag out of the church. At the beginning of the Reich Manual Skills Week in 1933, a priest in Kirchen decorated his parish house with two church flags. The local SS leader asked him also to show the swastika flag, but instead the priest took down his church flags without raising the swastika. Moreover, the local Catholic hospital, which had been flying the swastika flag, removed it. The HJ uniform and insignia also met with prohibitions. On June 4, 1933, in the town of Till, a school boy came in his HJ uniform. The priest made him take off his swastika arm band in order not to "disturb the mass". In the Rhineland, November 19, 1933, when a group of Hitler Youth appeared at mass in uniform, the priest asked them to wear coats over their brown shirts.

The nonrecognition of Nazi symbols sometimes extended to funerals. At Marienborn, a priest aroused the indignation of the SA at the funeral of one of their number by jerking down the hand of his acolyte when the assembled mourners gave the "Heil Hitler." At the burial of an SA man in the village of Mozingen, a priest complained about the pallbearers wearing brown pants. More striking in a way, was the case of the priest who had the swastika flag removed from the casket of an SA man before saying his blessing over it. Obviously, most Nazis did not think they were forsaking their faith when they joined the party or its formations; indeed, it is in a way not hard to see why they would angrily denounce their local priests on being denied sanction for National Socialist ceremonials: they had always assumed they could be both Catholic and Nazi, and yet the priest, by his reserve, implied that the two could not be reconciled.

Despite such occurences, local Nazis continually endeavored to involve the Church in Nazi ceremonials, or rather to superimpose their political rites on the liturgical rite. Sometimes, priests simply overlooked the presence of closed formations in church. In February 1934, in Marienborn, the local *Sturmbann* decided to celebrate the Heroes' Memorial Day by attending mass as a group. A representative asked the local priest, (the one who was later to jerk down his acolyte's hand), to commemorate the dead in his sermon. The priest refused saying he had spoken of that subject the previous week, as the SA man might have known had he been present at the sermon. Sunday came, and the SA sat through a sermon which in no way touched the subject they had assembled to commemorate. In Münster on "Youth Sunday", (October, 1933), when the *Jungvolk* came to Assistant Priest Flugge's church and almost filled it up, he simply ignored their presence, and directed his sermon to the Catholic youth group there.

Occasionally, a priest would take the offensive in this matter, as for example, in May 1934, in Bad Orb, where the BDM for the first time attended mass in uniform. In his sermon, the priest pointed out that the devil appears in many forms: sometimes in the form of wine, sometimes in the form of games, and sometimes in the form of a beautiful woman. Now, however, he very often appeared in uniform.

Pastor Droll decried most vehemently the ceremonials of the Harvest Thanksgiving. First, there was a closed procession to mass in the morning, which he denounced from the pulpit: "It is idiocy, it is a worldly celebration and not a church one. Even the Mother's League flag is there." His refusal to rearrange the afternoon devotion meant the festive procession could not be carried through uninterrupted. Then, on Sunday, October 8, 1933, he lashed the participants of the festive procession: "Shame, shame, and shame again to those who like vagrants took part in the procession. They may not participate in the mission." And he added that anyone who had taken part in the evening demonstration had taken communion unworthily.

In a few cases, Catholics intruded upon the National Socialist realm with symbols, greatly vexing the Nazis. The "Heil Loyalty" has already been mentioned. One priest renamed his girls' sodality, the *Marienkinder,* the *Bund Deutscher Marienkinder* and abbreviated it BDM, incurring Goering's ire in a subsequent directive. Catholic youth and workers' associations devised a parody of the SS oath and turned it to Christian purposes, a practice which made true Nazis boil.

The refusal to give his sanction to National Socialist ceremonials was an area of freedom from which a priest could hardly be dislodged. He could certainly be punished for attacks on the regime, and might possibly even be punished for acts of nonparticipation, but ultimately, no one could force him to take a positive attitude toward Nazism. Some priests, as early as the first year of the regime, articulated the feeling of being vulnerable to punishment, and yet chose, come what would, to hold on to their own opinions. "[I] will not change my mind, even if they stand [me] up against a wall." "They can put me in jail, but they can't change my mind." One priest, in 1933, publicly predicted a persecution of Christians within one year. It was true enough in his own case: he soon fled to the Saar to avoid prosecution.

The support of ecclesiastical superiors

The degree of opposition to the regime offered by Catholic clergy may have depended upon the initiative of their ecclesiastical superiors. From the reports assembled by the *Sicherheitsdienst, Oberabschnitt Rhein* in the summer of 1934, it appears that one of the cities providing an unusual number of denunciations was the episcopal see of Limburg.

Antonius Hilfrich, bishop of Limburg, adamantly opposed National Socialism.   No swastika flag flew over his cathedral.   In a pastoral letter, he attacked the educational policies of the regime. During the latter half of 1933, when the *Frankfurter Volksblatt* published a demand that the members of the Catholic youth organizations join the HJ, the local *Nassauer Bote* published a counterstatement by Bishop Hilfrich: "Remain true to your Catholic youth groups; the concordat protects you, and the bishops hold their hands over you!" Once, when an HJ member entered the cathedral in his uniform, the bishop could hardly contain his anger.   The suggestive point here is that the priests of his diocese seemed just as vigorously opposed to Nazi encroachment.   They attacked the regime for its policies on youth, and its connections with the "new heathenism".   In a sermon on April 22, 1934, a priest went more directly to the point, equating National Socialist youth organizations themselves with heathenism: "The national organizations are the new 'heathenism': Their members attend no church and seek after Nature."   The *Sicherheitsdienst* regarded the diocese as a seat of the "black reaction."[3]

The case of an elderly nun makes clear how different it was at St. Anna's Girls' Secondary School in Königstein in Taunus.   When greeted with a "Heil Hitler", a teacher, Mother Xaveria, retorted: "Stop the tomfoolery, you are just trying to show that you are in the BDM."   Once when the girls in her class had been particularly noisy before the beginning of instruction, with tears in her eyes the aging nun rebuked them: "You are behaving just like the new Germany." When she heard that some of her students had reported her remarks to Miss Wessling, a lay teacher, the nun told the girls in her class they ought to become washerwomen, because they were traitors just like Miss Wessling.   Miss Wessling was indeed reporting to the director of the school, Mother Julia, while the girls for their part reported to their BDM leader, who passed the word on to the *Ortsgruppenleiter* of the NSDAP, the latter in turn informing the mayor of Königstein. Without waiting to be summoned, Mother Julia and the prefect of the nunnery, Mother Bonaventura, presented themselves to the mayor. Mother Julia assured him that not only had she personally reprimanded Mother Xaveria, she had also requested the head of the order in Frankfort to warn Mother Xaveria against any future remarks and to threaten her with removal from teaching. The mayor, however, was not satisfied. He insisted upon her immediate dismissal from teaching and removal from the school. A few days later, Mother Julia informed him that his wishes had been met.[4]

The comparison between St. Anna's, and the bishop and clergy of Limburg may not be entirely fair. Catholic orders were especially vulnerable to punitive action because they depended upon voluntary contributions for their support, and had to eschew bad publicity; nor could a nun look to the support of loyal parishioners. The parish priest who had, on the one hand, the support of his bishop and, on the other, a loyal following in his parish was doubly protected from punitive actions.

If the bishop were sympathetic to the supposed aims of the regime, however, as was Archbishop Gröber of Freiburg,[5] the oppositional position of a parish priest could be vitiated. Following the signing of the concordat, and his negotiations with Buttmann, on June 28, 1933, the archbishop instructed the priests of his diocese "to avoid in sermon, catechetical instructions, as well as in organisational activity, and in private talks, everything that could be interpreted as criticism of leading personalities in state and community, or of the political views held by them." Similar instructions were issued by the bishops of Würzburg, Passau, and Paderborn. The instructions issued by Bishop Ehrenfried of Würzburg in July put it out of the province of the individual priest to criticize the actions of subordinate state officials whose "wrongful and interfering measures might militate against our cooperation with the national movement and disturb our sympathetic attitude towards it. It is not ... the duty of the individual priest to judge of such matters or to redress them ... Insofar as necessity arises, such questions will be dealt with by higher ecclesiastical authority."[6] In a few instances, bishops transferred priests who were too outspoken in their criticisms.[7]

The SD plan to silence priests

In June 1934, the *Sicherheitsdienst* prepared a report in which it set out the problems facing National Socialism in its dealing with the Catholic Church, and recommended steps to be taken toward the solution of those problems.[8] While the report reveals the constraints suffered by the Nazis in their dealings with the Catholic Church, it also reveals the redoubtable range of powers which Nazism had at its disposal.

As the report saw the problem, the Catholic Church was guilty of separatism: it had created a separate culture, and a separate social and political theory, and held the Catholic people in its own modes of thought, insulating them mentally from the totality of the people and its developing life. While Catholics might be "loyal to the state," their loyalty had always been mediated through the position of the Church, which had never been inactive politically. That mental separatism of German Catholics on occasion led to desires for separation from the Reich, or at least led German Catholicism to look for help from abroad. If the Catholic clergy in Germany had taken a position with regard to National Socialism, which itself derived from the spiritual act of uniting with the fate and developing life of the nation, the question of competence of the spheres of church and state would not have been so serious a problem. However, as it was, "the pushing back of political Catholicism [had to be] the fateful issue of the National Socialist movement, if it [was] to fulfill its historical tasks, the completion of the inner unity, and evolution of the *Volk*."

The Church knew, the report continued, that the opponent who had to build on new foundations was in the more sensitive position. For years, the Church had entrenched itself and supervised the participation of the Catholic in all spheres of life. Catholics were brought up with a "blindly subjective" reliance on their priests, and that fact limited the actions police could take against pastors. Jail, protective custody, and the concentration camp were to be avoided for fear of the negative effect of such measures upon the Catholic population; moreover, such steps were likely to make the priests appear as martyrs, and a public trial might be used by them to stage "innocence demonstrations."

The *Sicherheitsdienst* recommended a new series of actions in proceeding against clerical enemies of the state without "martyring" them. The basic policy behind the tactics was to drive the Church and the clergy out of the realm of "politics" and back into the realm of "purely religious" spiritual care. In acting against clergy, the police agency in question was to be certain to distinguish between actions dictated by the centrally controlled Catholic Action, and those which arose from the personal opposition of the priest to the regime. Since Catholic Action was so carefully camouflaged by religion that action against it was precarious, the immediate task was to take action against clergy personally opposed to the regime; defensive measures against Catholic Action would have to be of some other sort. The police should also distinguish between the "uncontrollable, silent influence" of a priest, and tangible acts of opposition.

The state did not have to remain defenseless against acts of opposition, and had a variety of means for proceeding against them.

In the first place, the SD report argued, an act of opposition deprived a priest of the protection of the concordat. The Führer had expressly stated at the time the document was signed that the concordat took the clergy out of politics, and placed the priest positively behind the National Socialist state. Clergymen who did not fulfill those stipulations would no longer enjoy the protection of the concordat.

Secondly, and more important, every parish priest held certain privileges granted by the state. Those privileges could be revoked. One such privilege was that of teaching religious classes in the confessional schools. No priest who in any way showed opposition to the regime should be permitted to continue in that capacity. Moreover, every parish priest in Germany received a salary from the state; assistant priests also received a public subsidy in the form of a parish tax. The state set certain standards for parish priests, such as the possession of an examination certificate from a German *gymnasium,* and just as the state could grant the permission to assume the duties of parish priest, it likewise could withdraw that permission.

Therefore the procedure throughout Germany was to be as follows:

1) *Any priest who opposed the regime was to be deprived immediately of the right to give religious instruction in the confessional*

schools.

2) *In more serious cases, the priest was to be summoned by the police and informed that he had been deprived of his salary and the right to remain in his parish. The final confirmation of that act had to be made before a court, but the proceedings were not public. Once confirmed by the court, the decision could not be appealed, and the prohibition was for life.*

Following his conviction, the priest had to reside at a distance from his old parish sufficient to insure that he would retain no influence over it. He retained his capacity as priest (from which in any case neither state nor Church can ever free him), and could say mass, but he was prohibited from the care of souls: he could neither preach, give instruction, hear confessions, nor maintain any sort of pastoral relations with any group whatever. He was to be kept under surveillance for six months, by which time it could be supposed that the new priest who had replaced him would have established himself and would, in concert with the higher authorities of the Church, wish to prevent the former pastor from resuming any influence over the parish.

The police were to make public announcements that they were going to take defensive measures against priests opposed to the regime, depriving them of permission to care for souls. However, reports in the press of specific actions were to be suppressed. Apparently, the *Sicherheitsdienst* expected the Catholic clergy to learn the state of affairs for itself, and the SD resolved to insure optimum destruction of morale by taking action suddenly, and simultaneously throughout the Reich against the most prominent opponents of the regime. Again, however, caution was enjoined to keep reverberations from disturbing the peace of the parish. Action was to be taken primarily against parishes having two or more priests, so that on the following Sunday mass could be said as usual. The *Sicherheitsdienst* calculated that the higher Church authorities, in the interests of the parishes, would provide for the continuation of the sacraments, but anticipated possible difficulties on the first Sunday following a punitive action.

3) *Should the church authorities attempt stopgap measures in the filling of vacancies in the parishes, the Regierungspräsidenten should assist the police in putting pressure on them, since they held*

the power to approve or disapprove of the new appointment and to grant or deny the salary.

4) A less drastic form of action was to call the priest to the police station and threaten him with proceedings. But even in this case, he was to be informed that he was forbidden to give religious instruction in the schools.

5) In the case of clergy who were members of orders, little difficulty was anticipated. In the first place, such clergy did not have the backing of a devoted parish. Moreover, the orders were themselves very sensitive to public opinion, inasmuch as they depended upon contributions for their support. The SD believed that the member of an order could simply be forbidden to preach, lecture, write, or leave his cloister. The order, insecure and lacking protection as it did, could be counted upon to force the individual priest to comply.

6) The Sicherheitsdienst expected its actions against parish priests to cause those not directly affected to exercise considerable restraint in their utterances. Depriving priests of their parishes was striking right at the core of their lives, and they could be expected to exercise discretion in order to retain their parishes, (which in fact many priests, though unalterably opposed to the regime, and not timorous, may have felt in conscience bound to try to do). Even the leaders of Catholic Action would have to restrain themselves because they would have cause to fear that their actions might also be labeled "personal" actions, and proceeded against.

The SD report then listed a number of clergymen who were to be proceeded against. Among them was the Jesuit priest Fritz Vorspel, whose Lenten sermon was quoted in the early pages of this chapter. The appropriate police officer was to inform the head of the cloister in question that Father Vorspel was not to be employed outside of the cloister in any way, and even inside the cloister could not preach or hear confessions of any persons not residents therein.

CHAPTER SEVEN

The Church Defines Its Position

The period of preparation, January to April, 1934

The German "defensive note" of January 14, 1934, protested *inter alia* the attitude of the younger clergy, who made "no secret of their dislike for the new Reich." Already, in Germany those spontaneous feelings were beginning to be shaped into a coordinated campaign to strengthen the loyalty of the laity, and their powers of resistance. The British ambassador later wrote that he had heard that the Papacy had given instructions to the Church to use the period between Christmas and Easter to prepare the laity for whatever resistance might later prove necessary: if the situation in Germany did not improve by Easter, dissent might become still more spirited. The ambassador's information coincides at least in part with later observations of the *Sicherheitdienst,* which found that the Catholic Church had used the months from January to April for "inner work." "Never before in so short a time, had so many missions and religious weeks of all sorts been held; never so many episcopal letters from the bishops, and sermons of prominent clergymen (Jesuits, above all) been delivered to the Catholic people, never had the Lenten sermons and Lenten episcopal letters been so forcible and adjuring, as in this year. It [was] a question of the inner mobilization of the Catholic laity."[1]

Among the more notorious demonstrations was a gathering of 14,000 Catholics on February 11, 1934, at the *Sportspalast* in Berlin, scene of many a Nazi rally. Erich Klausner, head of Catholic Action, addressed the crowd on loyalty and love for Church and Fatherland.[2] The bishops took an active role in creating the new mood. On January 14, 1934, the second Sunday after Epiphany, the bishops of Germany completed their instructions concerning matrimony with the reading of *Casti Connubii*, the encyclical of Pius XI which condemned forcible sterilization as contrary to natural law. The Reich minister of the interior protested to Cardinal Bertram as president of the Fulda conference, and in Würzberg the police confiscated the diocesan bulletin

91

containing instructions. On February 1, Cardinal Faulhaber attacked
the sterilization law directly. On February 24, the Pope himself
attacked racial pride as contrary to the Christian spirit. On March 1,
Cardinal Schulte denounced, as heathenism and apostacy from Christianity, religion based on blood and race. One month later, the bishop
of Münster, Count Clemens August von Galen, who was to become
the most prominent and effective German opponent of the Nazis,
attacked the neo-heathen doctrines of race and blood, and the attempt
to create a new religion alien to Christianity and alien to the Christian
past of the German people. "A delusion from hell is afoot which
could also mislead good people." Hold to the faith of your fathers,
he said, and "guard especially, Christian parents, the young who have
been entrusted to your care." Similar words had been chosen by the
bishop of Trier, Dr. Bornewasser, on the second Sunday after Easter:
". . . Catholic parents and educators: protect the youth entrusted
to you. You are responsible that they should remain faithful to God
and to His Holy Church. . . ."[3]

On January 24, Hitler had provided an added stimulus to these
efforts when he appointed Alfred Rosenberg, the chief Nazi advocate
of a religion of blood and soil, to supervise the spiritual education
of the National Socialist party. The Vatican recognized the appointment on February 7, by placing Rosenberg's *Myth of the Twentieth
Century* on the Index. That same day Cardinal Schulte had an interview with the Führer, during the course of which he asked Hitler
whether he identified himself with Rosenberg. Hitler replied that he
did indeed identify himself with Rosenberg, but not with the author
of the *Myth*. When pressed as to how that was to be explained, Hitler
blamed the bishops for attracting attention to the book by their condemnations.[4] During the course of that same interview, the cardinal
brought up the question of Catholic organizations, but the way in which
he did so demonstrated both his ineptness at diplomacy and the fact
that while the Church was in effect united in spirit, on specific matters
there remained divisions of opinion. Cardinal Schulte told Hitler that
the chief reason for the difficulties between Church and state arose
from the delay in working out the interpretation of Article 31. In the
cardinal's opinion, the best basis for a solution lay in changing the
existing organizations into organizations of Catholic Action, but without
the great scope which Erich Klausner, the present leader of Catholic

Action in Germany, had in mind. Rather, Cardinal Schulte thought that independent diocesan organizations should be organized, much as those favored by the Pope. When the cardinal gained the impression during the course of this interview that Hitler would agree to Catholic organization on this "purely churchly basis",[5] he was probably correct, but it is unlikely that he interpreted the Pope's position accurately. The Vatican did not propose to surrender the Church's rights to activities extending beyond the church doors. That was the basic point of contention.

The chief battle continued to be waged over the youth associations. On December 19, 1933, Schirach had scored a great victory. In consultation with Reichsbishop Müller, a Nazi clergyman charged by Hitler with "coordinating" the Evangelical Church, he obtained the incorporation of the Evangelical youth associations into the Hitler Youth. Now, the Catholic youth organizations stood as the last holdouts against the totalitarian claims of the Hitler Youth. The state began to intensify pressure. Ten days before the incorporation of the Evangelical youth, Hitler had proclaimed that confessional youth organizations had lost their right to exist and should disappear. In January 1934, a local Hitler Youth leader echoed the threat. In late January, Hitler Youth attacked groups of young Catholics assembled before the churches in Cologne. Early in February, the state police office in Düsseldorf prohibited to Catholic youth groups within the governmental region all public appearances and public activities. On the 23rd of that month, the German railways revoked the discount privileges formerly granted to members of Catholic youth groups. A regional Hitler Youth leader speaking in Cologne vowed that the Hitler Youth would not be satisfied until every German boy stood in its ranks. Schirach himself at Essen boasted that having overcome Marxism, the Hitler Youth would not stop in the face of the Catholic youth organizations. On March 27, he publicly predicted that the Hitler Youth would incorporate the Catholic youth organizations, which had no "right to lead a separate existence."

Schirach took a step toward making his prediction come true in March, by negotiating an agreement with Robert Ley, leader of the German Labor Front, which specified that boys under eighteen and girls under twenty-one years of age could be admitted to the Labor

Front only if they belonged to the Hitler Youth organizations. Since membership in the Labor Front was becoming increasingly essential for obtaining apprenticeship training and holding jobs in German industry, the threat was a trenchant one. A Catholic youth member was prohibited, by Schirach's decree of July 29, 1933, from simultaneously being a member of a Catholic youth organization and of the Hitler Youth. Now with the Schirach-Ley agreement in March, 1934, a young person not in the Hitler Youth could not join the Labor Front. Ley went on to extend the prohibition to adults on April 28, 1934, when he issued a decree of his own against simultaneous membership in the German Labor Front, and in denominational workers' associations. That decree was to prove more effective against the workers' associations than Schirach's decree had proved against the youth organizations, for it directly threatened the livelihood of the Catholic worker.

Early in February, Buttmann stopped off in Cologne and in Freiburg[6] to consult with Cardinal Schulte and Archbishop Gröber, and then proceeded to Rome, where he remained from the 6th to the 13th. His discussions with Cardinal Pacelli covering the gamut of disagreements between Church and state in Germany, evinced no progress. Cardinal Pacelli spoke of the possibility that the Pope would, by issuing a White Book, confront the world with the position of the Church in Germany. Buttmann warned that the German government would counter with a publication of its own proving political interference on the part of the Church. When adverting to the Rosenberg issue, Buttmann objected to the Church placing *Myth of the Twentieth Century* on the Index now, four years after its publication. Cardinal Pacelli retorted that the Pope was determined not to deliver the Catholic youth organizations to a Hitler Youth under the influence of Rosenberg. On February 15, Buttmann returned to Berlin where he sought out Papen. He told the vice-chancellor that in his opinion, the most difficult question in the whole complex of questions surrounding Catholic organizations was the question of the youth groups because the personal interest of the Pope was most clearly involved there.[7] On the 16th, he sought out Interior Minister Frick, who he found was having his own troubles with Goering.[8]

Papen set about to work out an agreement on the Catholic youth associations. From Schirach, he obtained a statement that the Hitler

Youth would guarantee to its Catholic members the opportunity for spiritual care by the Church, provided that the Church kept entirely out of politics. The Catholic youth organizations would be limited to the "purely religious" sphere, and the prohibition against double membership would be lifted. This meant, for instance, that Catholic youth would be released on the same afternoon as were the Evangelical youth, for special instruction by clergymen. The local Hitler Youth leader had the right to attend such instruction to make sure that it was strictly nonpolitical. The Catholic youth organizations would become mere sodalities, but at least the Hitler Youth agreed to encourage them in their work.[9]

The proposal was indeed almost gravely tempting, although it meant the end of Catholic youth organizations in their current form. The *Arbeitsgemeinschaft katholischer Deutscher,* (the Nazi front organization supported by Papen), had been arguing that with such an arrangment the Church could reach a greater number of young Catholics than it did through its own organizations. On the other hand, the education afforded Catholic youth in an afternoon's instruction would be far inferior to that implicit in the manifold experiences which could be offered within a meaningful youth group motivated by Christian principles. It was a question of quantity versus quality, always a perplexing matter for those involved in the care of souls.

Papen sent Schirach's proposal to Hitler, who took it up, with Ambassador Bergen, who happened to be in Berlin bearing proposals for a new concordat, and—or so Buttmann thought—trying to preserve his position, which Hitler was thinking about giving to Buttmann. Bergen pointed out that the Vatican was in a crusading mood and advised that when Buttmann made his next visit to Rome, he be prepared with some sort of proposals in order to ward off a conflict. Hitler agreed that Buttman could use Schirach's "concessions". Earlier in the month, from Rome, Bergen had proposed that Buttmann consult with Archbishop Gröber and then bring Cardinal Schulte in on any agreement reached; then, when Buttmann returned to Rome, he would be in a strong negotiating position. Buttmann did stop off at Cologne and Freiburg before proceeding to Rome, where he had talks with Cardinal Pacelli in mid-April.

Since the first of the year, Cardinal Bertram had been sounding out opinion on the position the Church should take concerning the Catholic youth organizations.   He initiated the dialogue at the beginning of January with a circular letter to all bishops and requested an answer by the 15th of that month to the questions he posed.   Rector Peter Heuser (of the *Jugendhaus,* in Dusseldorf) met in Berlin with a few diocesan *Präses* of the JMV, and Jacob Clemens, (general secretary of the JMV), met with a few others in Würzburg.   These groups worked out a fifteen-page statement of their position, based upon the teachings of Leo XIII and Pius XI, and prepared copies of the statement for Cardinal Bertram and for the Vatican.[10]

Cardinal Bertram's first question had asked whether the Catholic youth groups could be consolidated into a few major groups.   The Catholic youth leaders replied that such a consolidation was not desired by the Church and would be interpreted by its opponents as a sign of weakness.   The second question had asked what activities the Catholic youth organizations could surrender to the Hitler Youth without prejudice to their religious interests and obligations.   The Catholic youth leaders saw three regions in which the interests of the two overlapped: occupational education, physical education, and political education.   In the matter of political education, they were willing for the state to have charge of "national political education in the narrow sense", while the Church should retain the right to education in patriotic citizenship, and social consciousness.   As for occupational education, the Catholic youth leaders conceded to the state the right to direct vocational training and retained for the Church education in occupational ethics.   As for physical education, the Catholic youth leaders were willing that the state should take over competitive sports and defense-educational sports, but they were not willing that the Catholic youth organizations should be left "merely with rosaries and devotions"; they needed games, wandering, tent camps, swimming and scouting as means for fostering a living Christianity in young Christians.

The arguments the youth leaders advanced for retaining these activities revealed how deeply the spirit of community, originating in the youth movement, had penetrated the Catholic youth organizations and how thoroughly the spirit had been integrated into a scheme of Christian education.   The youth leaders argued that the state's recognition of the Church's rights to the religious education of youth implied also the necessary freedom and means for such an education. And as "all experienced youth workers" knew, the care of young souls required the community life provided by sports, wanderings, Home Evenings, and excursions. These made it possible to put life into the lessons provided through the "dry" methods of preaching and lecturing. Uniting into a *Bund* created a spirit of community, and a youth community based on Christian principles was far more than an incidental Christianity; monthly lectures and masses could not compare with "the growing power of Catholic community life." In public demonstrations and marches, the member proclaimed his faith before the world; his uniform was not mere clothing, it was a symbol of his confession of faith.

Cardinal Bertram's third question had asked what should be demanded if the government offered a comprehensive opportunity for pastoral care within the Hitler Youth. The Catholic youth leaders replied that, first of all, relations between the HJ and Catholic youth organizations had to be clarified, and the rights of the latter guaranteed. They rejected the totalitarian claims of the Hitler Youth, and as for an incorporation into the HJ, they looked upon that as a surrender to unbelief. Any agreement with the HJ should call for a cessation of statements by Hitler Youth leaders hostile to the Church, permission for Catholic members of the HJ to participate in religious events of the parish youth, and appointment of a trustee, by arrangement between the local HJ leadership and the parish clergy, to oversee pastoral care of the Catholic members. Interdenominational services had to be brought to a halt, and members of the HJ should be allowed to fulfill their religious obligations on Sundays and holy days.[11] General Secretary Clemens took the statement to Rome, where he remained from January 29 to 31. He was well-received, and the Vatican approved the youth leaders' position.[12] That may partially account for the adamant stand Cardinal Pacelli took in his interview with Buttmann during February; although looked at another way, the youth leaders' stand may have received such full support from the Vatican because it coincided with the views of the Pope.

Pius XI had the greatest affection for the youth organizations and their members, an affection which he soon demonstrated. In mid-March, Monsignor Klens of Düsseldorf, (who served as the *General-*

präses of the *Marianischen Jungfrauenverband)*, was in Rome on business for the *Katholische Jugend Deutschlands*, a committee composed of leaders from all Catholic youth organizations. Monsignor Klens petitioned the Pope for a statement supporting the youth organizations, and received in reply through Father Leiber, a Jesuit priest close to Cardinal Pacelli, that the Pope would speak to German youth. When the message came on Easter, it was a powerful one.

A crusading mood

On Easter Sunday, April 1, 1934, Pope Pius XI sent to Monsignor Klens an Easter greeting adressed to the Catholic youth organizations of Germany, written in his own hand.[13]   The greeting left no doubt where the Pope stood.

Beloved sons:

We received with inner participation, and with great satisfaction the expression of kind devotion to the vicar of Christ, and of steadfast loyalty to the Holy Church which you have conveyed to us. With inner participation, for you are in the forefront of those who have already made great sacrifices for their religious ideals and continue to make them daily. With great satisfaction, in the courage of belief which you demonstrate, and the truly supernatural spirit which inspires you. Despite all difficulties through which providence leads you, and against a propaganda working with both temptation and pressure for a new conception of life which leads away from Christ and back into heathenism, you have kept your oath of love and fidelity to the Savior and His Church and remain, for that reason, all the firmer in your devotion to nation and homeland, which you, as in past times, still now wish to serve in the closest union and selflessness.

We know about the position of the Catholic youth of Germany because of our responsibilities of pastoral care; and we know also that you are the great concern of your bishops. Your organizations shall likewise know that their cause is our cause. With fatherly love, we lead you under the cross of Christ, which shines from your banners, and from the heart, we send to you, to your parents and your families,

*as a source of strength and unshakable loyalty to the faith,
the requested Apostolic blessing.*[14]

On April 3, the Holy Father granted a special audience to approximately 200 members of *Neudeutschland* and 100 members of the *Sturmschar*. Again, he expressed his deep concern for them, his appreciation of the sacrifices they made, and pledged his support.

> *We know . . . that already many from your fair groups,
> the Sturmschar, Neudeutschland, and from the Jungmänner-
> verbänden, in general . . . have given proof of a heroic
> courage and martyr-like faith and loyalty . . . and tell to all
> what we tell to you: that we will do everything possible to
> care for you, and if necessary to protect you. . . . We see
> that you fight for us, and for the honor of the Church. . . .
> We will fight for you, whenever it is possible. . . . Yes, we
> will, whatever the cost, always speak the truth, and defend
> the truth, and defend therewith your rights, which are the
> rights of conscience. . . .*[15]

The results of Pius XI's Easter message were immediate. His message was read in all the churches, and copies were attached to the church doors. In many places, Hitler Youths and others tore them down; in Würzburg, Nazi demonstrators assembled before the residence of Bishop Ehrenfried, and jeered the message, line by line; (when the bishop replied from his window to insults, the mob smashed in his door); the local and regional restrictions of activity presumably may have been reprisals for the Pope's message. On April 2, the *Pfad-finderschaft St. Georg* of Hattenheim planned to appear on the playing field in uniform to welcome a group from the Saar, but, at midday, the *Ortsgruppenleiter* of the NSDAP ordered them not to appear in uniform, and with their flag. Before the end of the month, public apearances of the Catholic youth groups had been forbidden in the governmental regions of Kassel and Wiesbaden, and strictures tightened in the city of Munich. The message and its aftermath were, of course, primarily inspiriting to Catholic youth, and the new fervor rose again seven weeks later at Pentecost. At that time, youth leaders again made a pilgrimage to Rome and pledged their loyalty in the name of the entire Catholic youth of Germany, and upon their return set about having every member repeat the pledge for himself.[16]

Apparently, there was a great reservoir of commitment to be tapped. Late in March, the press service of the Reich Youth Leadership had released to the north German edition of *Völkischer Beobachter* an "Appeal to the Catholic youth" warning them that they ran the danger "in the eyes of the German Community of being regarded as saboteurs of German unity," and calling upon them to join the Hitler Youth and not to be held back by their clerical leaders.

> *The Volk wishes to hear from your mouths, Catholic youth, not from the mouths of your leaders and secretaries—who pressure you into your factional position and have demonstrated through their behavior and attitudes that they have no understanding of Germany and of the unity of the Reich— whether, and on what grounds, you intend to remain aloof from our great community. The whole Volk will pronounce its judgment on you. This judgment will be committed to history. Catholic youth, speak!*[17]

This assault hardly conformed to Hitler's instructions to avoid controversies with the Church, and telegrams went out ordering the postal service to stop delivery. Copies delivered by other means, however, got through, and they produced a reaction among the Catholic youth of the diocese of Münster. The lay leaders of the city's youth groups drew up a statement attacking the appeal for its insults to the honor of the Catholic youth groups, and for its attempt to drive a wedge between the members of those groups and their clerical leaders. The Catholic youth made a confession of loyalty to their clerical leaders and "fundamentally rejected the exclusiveness of the 'either-or" choice with which the HJ tried to present them. "The Catholic youth knows its way and its tasks. . . . It is only an expression of its own will, if its leaders will not surrender it in these difficult times." "The Catholic youth solemnly declares that it is from loyalty that it does not surrender its organizations and its leaders." The young people affirmed that they valued the educational functions of their organizations even more highly in these days, when attacks on the Christian confessions were producing confusion and insecurity in the young. Within three days, 10,000 young Catholics in the diocese of Münster had signed the confession.[18]

The religious demonstration in the diocese of Münster

Münster also saw the opening of a wave of religious demonstrations which served the dual purpose of reaffirming the loyalty of Catholics to their organizations and implicity protesting the repressive policies of the Nazi youth and workers' organizations. In Billersbeck, on April 15, 20,000 men and boys from the diocese of Münster gathered to celebrate the 1125th anniversary of the death of St. Ludger, "apostle of Saxony and Frisia" who had died there. Previously, the saint's death had been celebrated at the centenary, but not at the quarter century. The *Sicherheitsdienst* regarded the occasion as a mere pretext for a demonstration. It all began when the bishop of Münster, Count Clemens August von Galen, whom the SD regarded as "the most active bishop of the western region", issued an appeal to the men and boys of his diocese to come to Billersbeck to "present their confession of loyalty to the holy faith which they have inherited". The appeal was printed as a handbill and distributed throughout the diocese. Members of Catholic Action, (an organization of laymen who helped the bishops and priests), sought to interest participants. On the morning of April 15, the bishop performed mass in the cathedral at Billers -beck, and at 3:00 that afternoon, the men and boys assembled in the square to hear his speech, which was also broadcast over the radio. The *Sturmschar, Jungschar,* and *Gesellenverein* were there in uniform and bearing flags. This demonstration set the style for those which ensued in other regions of western Germany,[19] and these demonstrations were the cynosure in the conflict between Church and state in Germany through May and June.

CHAPTER EIGHT

The Church on the Offensive, May-June 1934

Diplomatic stalemate

In April, Minister Buttmann returned to Rome for another series of consultations between the 9th and 19th of that month. In his interview with Cardinal Pacelli on April 12, he presented a copy of Schirach's letter to Papen of February 20, with the assurance he had been empowered to negotiate on the proposals contained in it. Although the cardinal seemed very pleased with the letter and indicated he would present it to the Pope, he informed Buttmann that same evening that the proposals in the letter ought to be presented in a formal note from the German government before he and Buttman could negotiate on them: naturally a letter from Schirach did not constitute a formal proposal from the German government, and Buttman merely reworked Schirach's concessions into a government note before presenting it to Cardinal Pacelli as the basis for negotiations.[1] On April 18, Cardinal Pacelli presented him with two documents which seemed to shift the basis of negotiation back to the questions of working out a clear interpretation of Article 31 of the concordat and preparing a list of protected organizations. The arguments the Catholic leadership had put forth in answering Cardinal Bertram's inquiries in January were reflected in the proposals Cardinal Pacelli now presented to Buttmann. The Church left sports to the state, but on the other hand it listed as protected under Article 31 of the concordat those organizations, "such as *Deutsche Jugendkraft*", which were devoted to physical activity "according to Christian principles." The Vatican stipulated that the youth organizations had the right to wear uniforms and carry banners while going to church, and participating in processions, pilgrimages, patron saints' days, and other religious occasions, as well as at events which fell within the scope of their region of activity as it was to be defined in an agreement between the Holy See and the German government. The decree against double membership in the Hitler Youth and Catholic youth organizations was to be revoked. Organizations

103

formed on social and occupational lines, such as the *Gesellenverein,* were also entitled to the protection of Article 31.[2]

Buttman frankly told the cardinal secretary of state that his instructions confined his power of action to obtaining through the Pope the renunciation by the youth organizations of every form of activity not of a strictly religious nature. The leaders of Germany, he continued, considered the present period a transitional one. In time, the activities of confessional youth organizations would be limited to religion, and the groups mentioned in paragraph two of Article 31 of the concordat would disappear. Hitler intended not only to deny sports to organizations other than the Hitler Youth, but to deny them activities which resembled sports. If the Holy See could not agree to that, Buttmann said he did not know what would happen.[3]

The hopes aroused on both sides in the interview of April 12 were exposed as false by the Church's attempt to retain for the Catholic youth organizations the rights guaranteed by the concordat. Buttmann left for Berlin with agreement no nearer than it had been before his trip to Rome. To inform the German episcopate of the situation, on April 20, Cardinal Pacelli wrote Cardinal Bertram about the porposals exchanged and added that the Pope might now give to the bishops the task of negotiating directly with the German government, as Buttmann had suggested. However, the Pontiff's instructions to the bishops severely limited their scope of action: in accordance with local conditions, they were to present a conciliatory plan based upon the proposals already offered by the Holy See, pointing out to the German authorities that these represented all that in conscience could be conceded.[4] On April 30, the Vatican instructed its nuncio to assist the bishops in their negotiations with the German government.[5] The Pope was receiving numerous visits from German bishops, and their complaints about conditions in Germany angered him. On May 21, Cardinal Pacelli wrote to the nuncio that the Holy Father insisted that the bishops cede no rights guaranteed by the concordat.[6]

On June 6, Hitler was given a copy of a Vatican note of May 14, another document in the war of notes being waged by the two sides with an eye to eventual publication. This note, more than forty pages in length, reviewed the burdens of the Church in Germany and condemned the irreligiousness of persons near the head of government.

Of the many causes of conflict reviewed in this note, one stands out
as fundamental, for it defined the range of Church interests in a way
which was completely unacceptable to Nazi totalitarianism. Speaking
of the anti-Christian trend of education in Germany, the Vatican proclaimed that the Church could not limit itself to the "purely religious"
sphere, since to limit the Church to "purely religious" means in the
attainment of its goals was to regard it as a *societas perfecta,* which
it was not. Masses and sermons did not alone comprise a Christian
education. In pursuing "purely religious goals," in the education of
the younger generation in the spirit of Christian belief, the Church
must use means adapted to the needs of the young, even though these
means were "not purely religious in nature". The proximate goal of
the Church's education was a "religious life regulated in the spirit of
Christian belief", the fulfillment of "the whole religious man."[7] But
Nazism's pseudoreligion was quite as covetous of the whole man. As
Schirach wrote late that same year, the Catholic youth associations
had to disappear, since "by promises for a life beyond they tried to
hold the youth back from the disinterested surrender to the state. . . ."[8]

On June 5, the Fulda conference opened. The German bishops
discussed what position they would take in the coming conversations in
Berlin and designated as their representatives with the government
Archbishop Gröber, Bishop Wilhelm Berning, and Bishop Nicholaus
Bares. Those prelates later arranged to meet with representatives of the
government on June 25. From the Church's side, the choice was
an unfortunate one. Archbishop Gröber was an open admirer of
what he thought to be the policies of national renewal of the new
regime and had worked closely with Papen and Buttmann. Bishop
Berning had been appointed by Goering to the Prussian council of
state, an advisory body, and Bergen had noted that he possessed "a
gratifying understanding of the wishes of the government and the needs
of the new times."[9] Goering had opposed Bishop Bares' appointment to the See of Berlin, but the Vatican regarded him as a "strictly
ecclesiastical bishop."[10]

The episcopate went on to draw up a pastoral letter which condemned in strong terms Nordic paganism, attacks on the Church,
the circulation of Rosenberg's book in schools and in labor camps,
and the persecution of Catholic organizations. In order not to prejudice

the forthcoming talks, Bishop Berning proposed to Cardinal Bertram that the reading of the pastoral be delayed. Cardinal Bertram agreed, and the date for reading was set at July 1.[11]

Hitler attempted to appear conciliatory too. On June 27, he received the three representatives of the hierarchy, and promised that with a satisfactory conclusion of the negotiations he would issue a statement forbidding state and party to support neo-heathen movements. Such a statement was in fact prepared, but Hitler saw that it was carefully worded to refer to "state and party administrative offices," leaving Rosenberg, who did not occupy an administrative office, free to proselytize for neo-heathenism as he saw fit. On June 28, Rosenberg, disturbed by attacks by churchmen, went to Hitler to see what he should do. The Führer told him with great energy: "the churches must not be unneccessarily attacked (the Saar question!)," but he was not to flinch on fundamentals.[12]   That advice explains Hitler's temporizing efforts; his subsequent remarks at that interview reveal what the Church in fact would have to face. As he was talking to Rosenberg, the Führer pointed to the gray wall at the end of the garden and said, "Yes, it will all end up here, some day I'll have [Papen's] whole office rooted out." (Papen had made a recent speech at Marburg critical of the religious policy of the regime, and Hitler had had the author, Dr. Edward Jung, thrown in jail.) He was true to his word. In the Röhm purge, on June 30, 1934, Jung and Papen's press secretary were shot, and two of Papen's office secretaries were sent to a concentration camp. But Hitler was a flexible politician when it suited his policies, and a few days later he offered Papen the post as ambassador to the Vatican where he could have helped soothe feelings. Papen refused that appointment, but in August accepted an appointment as German minister to Catholic Austria.

Also killed in the Röhm purge were the leader of Catholic Action, Erich Klausner, whose last public action had been the organization of an assembly of 60,000 celebrants of a Catholic Day in the *Hoppegarten* in Berlin on June 24,[13] and the lay leader of the DJK, Adalbert Probst. That Hitler should have ordered, or allowed those murders at a time when he was assiduously preserving relations with the Church may seem to require some explanation; however, we can only speculate. Probst may have been murdered because he was the highest nonclerical leader with the JMV. Erich Klausner's murder was probably the Nazi reaction to Catholic religious demonstrations in the Rhineland, which the *Sicherheitdienst,* rightly or wrongly, attributed to the co-ordinating efforts of Catholic Action.

Demonstrations in the west German dioceses

The demonstration on April 15 in the diocese of Münster had been a foretaste of what was to come. During May and June, religious activity inside and outside of the churches increased in an ever-rising crescendo. In Trier, the Catholic youth had planned a torchlight procession for Saturday evening, May 5. The procession was to move from the cathedral, through the city, to the Benedictine Abbey of St. Matthias. On May 3, police withdrew permission for the procession. A large crowd gathered before the cathedral on May 5 anyway, but the bishop, who had been warned by the police, ordered them to disperse.

The following day, Sunday, May 6, witnessed processions in the cities of western Germany. In Limburg the Catholic youth of the diocese gathered on the occasion of the Dom Bosco celebration. Over 4,000 young men marched, and the bishop, Antonius Hilfrich, marched among them. They assembled to hear him speak, and the topic of his speech revealed clearly what the march was all about. The topic was loyalty. "I travel now to Rome to the Holy Father. What shall I bring him from you?" The young men answered in a great shout, "Our loyalty!"[14] In the diocese of Mainz, 7,000 men and boys assembled to hear their bishop.[15] The Catholic youth of Hamburg likewise assembled to hear their bishop, Dr. Berning of Osnabrück. The *Sicherheitsdienst* was rather surprised that a demonstration occurred in Hamburg, and that Bishop Berning spoke at it, facts which it interpreted as evidence that the demonstrations proceeded according to a central plan. Bishop Berning's speech was much more reserved than those of the other bishops, however, reflecting perhaps a desire not to prejudice his acceptability as a negotiator in future dealings with the government.[16]

But the largest demonstration occurred in Essen, where 30,000 men and boys assembled on the Adolf Hitler Plaza. The demonstration revolved around the displaying of a picture of Mary, which was proclaimed a holy picture of "Our Beloved Lady in Need." The event was well publicized. The laymen of Catholic Action went from house to house, and to the Catholic organizations to recruit participants; invitational sermons were preached in all churches on the morning of the event, and the program of the celebration was distributed. The *Essener Kirchenblatt,* with a circulation of over 10,000, published an appeal to participate. Processions from the individual parishes followed their pastors to the Adolf Hitler Plaza, where a wall of church flags and organizational banners were displayed. The holy picture was presented, a prayer in plain chant was recited, and then there were two speakers. The second speaker referred to the picture of "Our Beloved Lady in Need" as "the symbol of our time."[17]

The police took action to prevent a recurrence of such public processions by members of Catholic organizations. Henceforth, uniforms and organizational flags were to be permitted only within the church, and on church grounds. In public, only "processions of a traditional, customary sort" were to be allowed. Instead of bringing such appearances to a halt, these prohibitions merely transformed them. Organizational uniforms and flags were no longer in evidence on public streets and public plazas, but they were all the more conspicuous within the churches and on church plazas. Traditional religious feasts were celebrated by procession and pilgrimages on a scale which was quite out of the ordinary. Some localities which had been minor sources of pilgrimage suddenly became major ones, and Catholics began to use a new term to refer to these pilgrimages: *Glaubensfahrten.* "So the prohibition is totally evaded, and the demonstrations are even bigger and more forceful than previously", lamented the *Sicherheitsdienst.*[18]

On May 13, there were celebrations in honor of Mary in Essen, Aachen, Cologne, and in the dioceses of Limburg and Mainz.[19] But May 15, the Feast of the Ascension provided the occasion for new mass demonstrations, staged now within and on church grounds. In Cologne, approximately 20,000 young men came to the cathedral to hear a sermon by Dr. Teusch and to make a solemn pledge of loyalty led by the priest in the pulpit with the assembled worshippers responding. "Catholic young men, what do we send Christ?" Answer: "Our loyalty!" Question: "What do we send to the Holy Church, what do

we send to the Pope in Rome?" Answer: "Our loyalty!"[20] Father
Teusch's sermon was printed as a handbill entitled "Young Church",
and given a mass distribution. Its echoes were heard in pulpits
throughout the land. It contained some striking phrases: "As long
as there is German fidelity, as long as the word of a chancellor has
value, as long as treaties are holy, there will be rights for the Catholic
youth in Germany!" In Düsseldorf, there was a substantial demonstration featuring the youth, although it was not on the scale of some
of the other cities since the Church's influence "in the public field"
was not as great there.[21] On the same day, May 15, the Düsseldorf
group of the JMV made a pilgrimage to the Madonna of Altenberg.[22]

The largest demonstration to be held up to that time occurred
on May 15, the Feast of the Ascension, in the diocese of Aachen.
Approximately 40,000 young people assembled for a pilgrimage to
the Holy Picture of the Mother of God at Aachen. The bishop invited the entire youth of his diocese, and some came from as far as
75 kilometers away. Girls came by special trains, the young men
made a night pilgrimage on foot or bicycles. The young people of
each city of the diocese were assigned a church in the city of Aachen
at which they received communion.[23] Then the youth assembled in
the court between the cathedral and *Rathaus*. The holy picture was
brought out, and the bishop, Dr. Joseph Vogt, appeared and was
greeted with the "Heil loyalty" of thousands. The bishop celebrated
a pontifical mass and delivered an address which he concluded by
exhorting all to "remain loyal to our church." Next, the bishop
received some 1,000 or 2,000 youth leaders in the largest pastors'
home in the city. Following another address by the bishop ("Hold
out, my dear leaders, come what may! . . . May your power grow
and your young strength become greater. . ."), the boy and girl youth
leaders made a confession of loyalty to the Church on behalf of the
members of their groups. At noon, an hour's devotion to Mary was
held in the great court with 40,000 persons participating.

These were the momentous demonstrations, but throughout the
western region of Germany, mass gatherings on a smaller scale were
held at the local level. The JMV, apparently from the Koblenz
region, made a pilgrimage in May with 5,000 participants. Two
hundred young people made a pilgrimage from the Rheingau to

Marienthal. An SA man, standing outside a Catholic family's house, overheard a girl say of a pilgrimage to Marienthal that she had felt more edified spending a half hour there than a year contemplating "the fraud," an apparent reference to Nazism. In Gravenbroich, in the diocese of Cologne, 3,500 young people gathered for a confession of loyalty. "The young Church is loyal to the death," the priest said in his address to them, "even if the way of loyalty is hard." Fulda saw two loyalty demonstrations of Catholic youth during the month; one of which drew 3,000 participants. On May 23, 4,000 members of the JMV of the Trier region made a pilgrimage to the Eberhard cloister. On that same day, 3,000 men and young men of the diocese gathered for a demonstration in the cathedral court.[24] The police authorities for the Trier region retaliated on May 26 by restricting Catholic youth groups to religious activities.[25]

The JMV everywhere engaged in pilgrimages. The groups of a stipulated region would come together at a central meeting place and then proceed to a place of pilgrimage in the locality. On Sunday May 27, for example, the Cologne group led members from thirteen other regions on a pilgrimage to Altenberg. General Secretary Clemens delivered the sermon to the 2,500 young men assembled there.[26] Meanwhile, the *Gesellenverein* was making pilgrimages of its own. On Sunday, May 6, 4,000 journeymen from the diocese of Trier came by special trains to participate in a great procession to the grave of Father Kolping, the "workers' priest," at the *Minoritenkirche* in Cologne. On May 13, 2,000 came from the Limburg diocese, and on Sunday, June 3, 1,500 from the diocese of Münster. During the month of May, nearly 50,000 journeymen made the pilgrimage.

May 31 was the feast of Corpus Christi, and the processions for the occasion were far larger than had been customary in the past. This was partly due to intensive work on the part of Catholic Action, which prepared pamphlets that the lay helpers distributed from door to door and to the Catholic organizations.[27] In the diocese of Mainz, approximately 30,000 members of the Catholic organizations marched on the Catholic youth playing field. A representative of the JMV, and a representative of the girls' organization pledged their loyalty to the bishop in the name of the assembled youth. The bishop, Dr. Ludwig Maria Hugo, delivered a speech in which he praised the role of the Catholic youth in Italy, implying that Germans might learn something from the situation there. Mussolini, he said, had told the Pope that the religious youth were the mainstay of the state.[28]

On Sunday, June 3, several thousand young men from those portions of the dioceses of Mainz, Limburg, and Trier which were contiguous to the Rhine made pilgrimage to Rochuskapelle bei Bingen. That day, groups of the JMV from the diocese of Cologne who had not yet been on pilgrimage set out on one with 2,000 young people participating. Assistant Priest Hochmann of Cologne-Deutz spoke to them of loyalty: "Our vow, our common oath before the picture of Mary is then; We, the young Church, will be true, true to the death!"[29]

Two days later, on June 5, in connection with the opening of the Fulda conference of bishops, a large pilgrimage of faith brought 20,000 participants to the cathedral and cathedral plaza at Fulda. Some of the pilgrims came from distant points by special trains. With the cathedral lit by floodlights, that evening, the bishop of Rottenburg, Dr. Johannes Sproll, spoke of the duties of the Catholic young man. His motto was "Fearless and Loyal!" and the theme of resistance was clear:

> *Loyal we want to be, for loyalty is a German virtue. . . .*
> *Be loyal, my dear Catholic youth, to the resolutions and vows*
> *you took in holy hours [first communion and confirmation]*
> *. . . . Fearless, that is the other part of our motto. Fearless, we*
> *bishops also wish to be. We use fearless men not only in the*
> *field, when bullets fly and grenades burst, we use them also*
> *when it is a matter of fighting in God's host. Also in the*
> *army of our King, Christ, we use fearless fighters. Such we*
> *wish to be, every day of our life. Heroism may come many*
> *times.*

Then the bishop led the assembled devout in a confession of faith.[30]

On June 10, another great faith pilgrimage united 20,000 men in, and in front of, the cathedral of St. Norbert in Xanten. The occasion was the 800th anniversary of the death of the saint, who had been born in Xanten and served as archbishop there. In the morning, Bishop Galen of Münster performed a pontifical mass for 8,000 or 9,000 persons within the cathedral, while another 6,000 young men in front of the cathedral participated by means of loudspeakers. At noon, a great youth demonstration took place at the cathedral, where 12,000 young Catholics from the surrounding villages converged to make a pledge of their loyalty. In all, 20,000 young men stood before the cathedral. When the towering and massive figure of Bishop Galen appeared before the cathedral, a great cheer went up. A young man stepped to the microphone: "We are glad that we may find ourselves here by the thousands, and that in our midst wave banners which bear the insignia of Christ." Bishop Galen addressed them. At Easter, he had been in Rome, he said; the Pope had praised the German nation, but he also made known his concern for the Catholic youth of Germany, The religious struggle in Germany filled him with sorrow. So too, he said, the efforts to import a heathen doctrine had greatly concerned the bishops meeting at Fulda a few days before: "All bishops are, as I am, full of love for the Catholic youth. We all have trust that the Catholic people, and the Catholic youth under the leadership of the bishops will remain true to Christ and their Church." At the conclusion of his address, a great cheer again went up. Then, 20,000 young Catholics raised their hands before the bishop and pledged their loyalty.

During the month of June the workers' associations of the Rhenish dioceses began making local pilgrimages. On June 17, while the workers of the northern part of the archdiocese of Cologne participated in a great celebration at Werden, near Essen, the groups from the southeastern part of the archdiocese made a pilgrimage to Bödingen; in the southwestern part of the archdiocese, the workers went to another local place of pilgrimage. The procedure was the same in the diocese of Aachen.

Large scale pilgrimages were made in the latter part of the month to Werden and Marienthal. The dioceses of Mainz and Limburg staged three pilgrimages to Marienthal on June 24, June 29, and July 1. These pilgrimages to Marienthal were not on the scale of those of Fulda, on June 5, Xanten on June 10, or Werden on June 17; but, two of them were marked by the presence of a bishop: the bishop of Mainz, June 24, and on the first of July by the bishop of Limburg.

The greatest celebration of all was that staged at Werden, which from June 17 to July 1 celebrated the 1125th anniversary of the death of St. Ludger, "apostle to the Saxons and Frisians." The workers' organizations opened the great celebration with their gathering on June 17; on June 23, the *Gesellenverein* made an evening pilgrimage followed late that night by the Catholic clerical workers' organizations; and on the following day, the *Akademikervereine* made theirs. The Catholic youth came on June 29, and on June 30, the Catholic women teachers' league of Essen and its environs.

The opening pilgrimage, that of the Catholic workers, began with a pontifical mass sung by Bishop Galen on the morning of June 17. Following the mass, the workers proceeded in a solemn procession through the streets of Werden. At around 2:30 that afternoon, 20,000 Catholic workers from all parts of the Rhineland and Westphalia crowded into the plaza before the abbey, where Bishop Galen addressed them with what the SD characterized as the sharpest attack on the National Socialist movement ventured since the seizure of power, and as an open incitement to resist the Labor Front; following this, a speaker led the assembled workers in prayer.

> *Speaker*: *Protect our people from force and unjust treatment.*
> *The People*: *We pray You, hear us.*
> *Speaker*: *We implore you to grant the leaders of our people the spirit of righteousness and love.*
> *The People*: *We pray You, hear us. . . .*

In closing, the throng repeated their heretical version of the SS oath with the last line altered to a pledge to the kingdom of Christ, (that same day a workers' pilgrimage in the southeastern part of the archdiocese of Cologne had also adopted the "borrowed" pledge). This day at Werden had been no ordinary religious celebration. The number of participants, and the zeal of the workers gave it something of the character of a political rally. Many came besides the 10,000 or 12,000 members of the workers' associations, bringing the total number of participants to nearly 30,000.[31] Whenever the leaders of the workers' associations appeared, the workers greeted them with storms of applause; Bishop Galen's address was frequently interrupted by cheers and clapping. Moreover, the proceedings were filmed, and within a week the film was making the rounds of the Catholic organizations in Essen.

The Catholic clerical workers' organization was the next arrival in Werden, with approximately 2,000 from the cities in the region meeting at 2:00 on the morning of June 24, and making their way with torches through the streets of the city to the abbey. Their president, Father Albord, in his sermon, touched on a source of anxiety which must have brought many of the pilgrims there, when he said that their prayers would accompany the German bishops, especially in these next days as they negotiated over the implementation of the concordat. Next, on Sunday, June 24, came the *Akademikervereine,* led by the Essen *Ortsgruppe,* and on the same day the *Gesellenvereine* of the Ruhr region, came 4,000 strong to "make their pledge of loyalty to the faith."

The Catholic boys had their turn on June 29, the feast of Peter and Paul, when 50,000 to 60,000 boys and young men, 25,000 of them members of the JMV, gathered in Werden. The JMV served as the core, but a wide appeal had been made to all Catholic youth to turn out. One of these appeals issued by the regional *Präses* and published in the *Essener Volks-Zeitung* on the morning of June 29, stressed the relevance of the demonstrations to the negotiations in Berlin. "The pilgrimage takes on a special significance due to the negotiations over the Catholic youth. We pray for a good outcome. . ."[32]

Three great columns of youth marched from Essen to Werden. Although in this region youth group uniforms were no longer allowed in public, many groups managed distinctive dress, displaying for example white shirts and black short trousers (JMV), or white shirts and grey trousers (*Neudeutschland Bund*); and the flags of the *Gesellenverein, St. Georg Pfadfinderschaft,* the *Sturmschar,* and the *Neudeutschland* were there. The *Neudeutschen* were heard singing a song with the appropriate lines: "And when they strike us down, we fight like cats!" The young people crowded into the plaza before the abbey, where a speaker led them in a prayer asking God to fill the leaders of the people with fear of Him, and obedience of His law, and to fill them with the spirit of righteousness and love. ("A boy who takes part in such things," said an SD report of the event, "is spiritually lost for the new Germany.") After this came a sermon by the Jesuit, Father Asch, a leader of the *Neudeutschen*: "Church or nation first? For us there is only One. Christ! Christ first in all, and before all."

Although there had been rivalry between the *Neudeutschen* and the JMV, it was nowhere in evidence now; "Thank you, Catholic JMV leaders," said Father Asch, "for your selfless work, for without you, our youth would not be so Catholic as they are today." A member of the JMV stood before the auxiliary bishop of Cologne, Dr. Wilhelm Stockums, and in the name of all present swore "Loyalty to Christ, loyalty to Germany, loyalty to Rome"; the assembled youth then sang the metamorphosed SS oath; and, finally, the bishop came forth to take their pledge of loyalty on behalf of the archbishop, Cardinal Schulte, and reminded the young men that they had also pledged their loyalty in Rome, and that the Pope had told them "your cause is our cause." The 50,000 then recited a confession of faith, raising their right hands at the end of the line "for the Kingdom of Christ and a new Germany."

In conclusion, the clerical leaders of the JMV of Essen addressed himself to the bishop on behalf of his group: "Your Excellency, you proceed now to Cologne. Tell his Eminence the Cardinal that the Catholic youth of Essen—no, . . . of the whole industrial region . . . *holds out until the final victory."* Another priest read two telegrams from the Catholic youth, one to the Pope, and the other to Bishop Bares in Berlin. To the Pope, they wrote: "The Catholic youth of Essen, 25,000 strong, gathered at the grave of the apostle of the Germans, St. Ludger, sends greetings in unbroken loyalty to Your Holiness, and requests Your blessing." To Bishop Bares, they wrote: "25,000 Catholic youth of Essen-Werden greet Your Excellency. They pray and supplicate for successful negotiations true to Church and Fatherland." Although addressed to Bishop Bares, the SD correctly regarded the telegram as intended for the Reich government as well, to let it know what stood behind the bishops in their negotiations.[33]

The final pilgrimage was made on June 30, the night of the Röhm purge, by the Catholic women teachers league of Essen and its environs. This league had been "coordinated" to National Socialism during the past year, but the technique which the Nazis had found so successful in dealing with other associations, and which proved efficacious in dealing with the men teachers organization, had failed here. The women continued to hold monthly religious gatherings to which they invited speakers, often enough Jesuits, who were particularly feared by the Nazis. "So it occurred," reported the SD, "that the Catholic women teachers, the bearers of *völkische* education ... dared to put themselves into the arena of the protest demonstrations of Werden," at a time when the men teachers organization cautiously stayed away. The women teachers assembled before the abbey at Werden at 10:00 p.m. on June 30, where a speaker led them in a prayer that God should grant the nation's leaders the spirit of truth and wisdom, and that the people should be protected from unjust treatment and force; they prayed for all who would be called to sacrifice their lives, and that their people might keep the Catholic schools, and that German youth should have Christian morality and the courage of faith.

The SD strategy against the teachers revealed again the coercive power available to the Nazi state, power which could often be exercised silently. Here, in the women teachers league, was an organization which had maintained itself in spite of its supposed "coordination," and while outwardly "coordinated" somehow sustained an informal organization, and a vital group consciousness. Still, the SS had a way to deal with it. The school authorities were ordered to prepare lists of those Catholic women teachers who belonged to the Catholic religious group, and find out which ones had participated in the pilgrimage. When the "cliques" of teachers had been uncovered, they were to be broken up by sending the teachers out of the city into the provinces, younger teachers of a different frame of mind were to be brought in to replace them; in order to minimize their influence on the young, the exiled recalcitrant teachers were not to be permitted to stay with the same class for more than one year.[34]

The *Sicherheitsdienst* regarded all of the processions and pilgrimages of the months of May and June as demonstrations of protest against the prohibitions of double membership by Ley and Schirach, and as part of a vast move to bring pressue to bear on the government in the negotiations with the hierarchy in the last days of June.[35] The SD looked upon Catholic Action as the coordinating agency for mobilizing the youth and workers' organizations,[36] although it imputed much to the organizations' own leaders.[37] There apparently was no certain evidence that Catholic Action was the catalyst the SD claimed it to be, but the suspicion probably motivated the murder of its leader,

Erich Klausner.[38] That selective murders would no more deter the faithful than had efforts at "coordination" was illustrated by the commemorative services which the JMV arranged for Probst, lay leader of the DJK, who also died in the Röhm purge (see p. 106 above). In Frankfort alone, 2,200 young people and 400 adults came to the cathedral at 5:00 a.m. on July 18 for a Requiem Mass and special prayers; the same mass was being said throughout the land.[39] That their death could be ritualized reminds us what depths of persecution were yet to be reached in the undifferentiated proceedings of the concentration camps. This was not to be the case with Probst, who would not be forgotten as long as there were Catholic youth groups.

The SD plans a counteroffensive

In the summer of 1934, the SD pondered what action should now be taken against Catholic organizations, and what should be done to prevent a recurrence of the epidemic religious fervor of May and June. The central office of Catholic Action, the SD was convinced, had brought together and mobilized the youth and occupational organizations, and had worked out the format of the huge demonstrations.[40] Extirpation was in order.[41] The same was true of the central offices of the Catholic organizations[42] whose leaders were traitors, although their "undoubted direct connection with the traitors of June 30" could not be proved.[43]

The central office of the JMV, as well as the regional offices, were all to be dissolved. The *Sturmschar, Deutsche Jugendkraft,* and *St. Georg Pfadfinder* were to go, as were the occupational organizations. The youth organizations founded upon occupational lines, such as the *Gesellenverein, Werkjugend,* and *Neudeutschland* were also to disappear, and the chief lay leaders of the youth organizations brought into the *Arbeitsdienst* in order to "educate" them in the spirit of the *Volk* community. The property of the proscribed organizations would become the property of the German Labor Front and Hitler Youth. To offset the loss, compensation might be offered the local bishop in the form of a mortgage on which he would be paid interest. Buildings owned by organizations might be retained by the Church provided they were devoted to "purely religious" purposes. The Church could retain its organizations based upon sex and age, that is, sodalities for

men, for women, for boys, and for girls.   But those organizations
were to devote themselves to "purely religious" goals and were to be
forbidden to engage in sports, or occupational or patriotic education.
No organizations were to be allowed any activities outside of their
parish.   Organizational publications were to be prohibited.   Organizational flags should likewise be prohibited except for certain "con-
secrated" flags stipulated in canon law.   Insignia and uniforms were
not to be tolerated outside of the church grounds, even in the cases
of processions and pilgrimages.[44]

Not all of these plans were carried out as easily as they were for-
mulated.   The central office of Catholic Action was not abolished until
1938,[45] and the central offices of the youth and occupational organizations were eliminated only after local dissolutions had eaten away
the foundations on which the central offices rested.   The great blows
to the JMV were the dissolutions of diocesan organizations.   The end
result was the same, but the destruction of the Catholic organizations
proved to be more complex, and involved a greater variety of coercive
powers than the SD had foreseen.

As for processions and pilgrimages, the SD determined that they
should be limited to participants from the parish of their origin.   The
parish priest was to be held solely responsible for the activities of the
Catholic organizations.   When it was necessary to proceed against a
priest, that would be done according to the plan by which a priest
could be excluded from religious instruction in the schools as a milder
measure, or as an extreme measure could be prohibited by the state
from having anything to do with the care of souls in any German
parish.   (See pages 86 - 89.).   Religious processions were to be permitted outside of the church grounds only when they were traditional,
as on Corpus Christi, Ascension Day, All Saints Day, and in the case
of funerals.   Such processions were not to go beyond the confines
of a parish and were to be held only for the members of the parish
itself.

Pilgrimages would be permitted only when led by the pastor, or
his duly authorized representative.   Pilgrimages by, and for individual
organizations were to be disallowed.   The pastor was to write to the
police authorities at the intended destination informing them of the
place of origin of the pilgrimage, the number of participants, and the

proposed itinerary through the streets.   It was up to the pastor to work out the day of his arrival with the custodians of the shrine.   The custodians were to take care that no more than one group, and that one always from a single parish, should proceed to the spot on any one day.[46]

With this program of repressive actions, many of which authorized the local police to deal with the problem by simply refusing permission to use the public streets, pilgrimages and processions could not as easily—if they could at all—take the form of rallies and demonstrations of protest.[47] These restrictions severely limited the ability of the Church to mobilize significant numbers of people and bring them together for a specific purpose.   By 1938, the *Sicherheitsdienst* could boast that one of the great pilgrimages of 1934 which had drawn 40,000 participants, now comprised little over one hundred.[48] Yet, the struggle to confine the Church, and the complaints of the police, would continue down to the fall of the Reich.   Reports from *Gau* Baden in April 1944 complained that important party members were still participating in religious celebrations—an *Ortsgruppenleiter* marched in a procession bearing the flag behind the priests, and another Nazi bore the crucifix.   Moreover, the priests were now using funerals as the occasions to make public speeches.   And, as a report from 1943 pointed out, the longer the war lasted, the more the people turned to the Church.

CHAPTER NINE

The June Agreement

Provisions of the draft

Early in July 1934, *Junge Front* published a note to contradict rumors concerning the recent negotiations between the representatives of the Reich government and the hierarchy. The truth was, the journal said, that the Catholic organizations, especially the youth organizations, would not be limited to church and sacristy, but would be allowed scope for their efforts in the work of building up *Volk* and Fatherland.[1] The editors' trust was misplaced. The negotiating bishops had surrendered nearly everything that the Papacy had fought to retain for the youth interests and had left the impression with the Reich negotiators that approval by Cardinal Bertram would follow as a matter of course.[2]

The draft agreement, and the corollary oral agreements would have completely altered the nature of the JMV. The document comprised two parts: first, a list of the organizations falling under the protection of the concordat; and secondly, a section setting out principles for the execution of Article 31. Part one, the list of protected organizations, was divided into two sections: Section A listing those organizations described in paragraph one of Article 31, organizations serving "exclusively religious, purely cultural and charitable purposes" (named here were charitable organizations, organizations supporting missionary activity, and the sodalities); and Section B, the organizations subsumed in paragraph two of Article 31, which protected organizations serving "other purposes," such as social or professional interests ... provided they guarantee[d] to carry on their activity outside any political party." Here, a single association was named, the *Kolpingswerk*[3]; the second paragraph of Article 31, the great shield with which the Papacy had guarded the youth and workers' associations, was simply cast aside.

In return for this sweeping concession, the state did guarantee to the organizations listed as protected under paragraph one of Article 31 "the requisite freedom for the carrying out of their tasks." Such

121

groups should not be forced into state organizations, nor deprived of their property; they had the right to recruit members, and their members could wear brooches and bear flags on certain religious occasions. On the other hand, the state reserved the right to investigate those organizations to insure that they confined themselves to their proper sphere as defined by the concordat. The organizations were, as a matter of principle, to be based on parish and diocese, and any supra-diocesan leadership required an agreement between the government and the hierarchy.

The bishops were to do away with the workers' and youth associations as they then existed. Occupational associations were to be incorporated into Catholic Action, and their vocational bases dissolved within one year. The bishops were to take care that Catholic Action served only nonpolitical goals and were to depoliticize the status and personnel of the incorporated occupational bodies. The stipulation that leaders of such organizations should be men who could be counted upon properly to circumscribe the activities of their groups meant that officials with a history of political activity were to be purged. The draft agreement was not so specific on the fate of the youth associations, but did clearly state that physical education was the affair of the state, which unquestionably entailed the end of the DJK. Foreign ministry records concerning the oral discussions reveal that some sort of future was envisioned for the Catholic youth groups, provided that they delimited themselves to moral and religious education.[4] In order to avoid unfortunate incidents, the bishops agreed that during the summer of 1934 they would forbid Catholic youth groups to hold tent camps and to wear uniforms; Schirach, who participated in the negotiations personally, gave assurance that the Hitler Youth would take a friendly attitude toward Catholic youth on wanderings and on other occasions, as long as they were led by a priest and seeking only 'moral" or "religious" benefits. Both he and the representative of the Labor Front agreed that when the draft agreement came into effect the Hitler Youth and Labor Front would rescind their decrees against double membership.[5]

The Vatican rejects the draft

The June agreement, which would almost certainly have been rejected by the Pope in any case, came to him at the time of the murders of Erich Klausner and Adalbert Probst, and the prospects grew even darker, when late in July Austrian Nazis murdered Chancellor Dollfuss. Ambassador Bergen wrote at the end of July that the Pope would not accept the draft agreement, which was already under attack by some of the German bishops, nor did he wish to resume negotiations. The Vatican did finally take up the subject again with a note to the German government on September 2 which Bishop Berning had requested as a support to the position of the negotiating bishops,[6] who were now being required by the Pope to undo what they had done. The Vatican note stated that the views of the bishops had only recently been received, and that an assessment of those views, and a study of the report of the negotiating bishops had led the Holy See to conclude that the concessions offered by the Reich government in the June draft fell short of those contained in the concordat itself, and therefore hardly constituted a valid interpretation of Article 31. The draft agreement would have to be modified, and the episcopal mediators were in a position to comment in detail on the necessary changes. The Holy See was willing to incorporate occupational organizations into Catholic Action and to deny these bodies involvements which were incompatible with Catholic Action ("professional, trade union and party-political activities"), but it was not willing simply to assimilate them to the general lay groups for men, women, boys, and girls, as provided in the June draft. As for the youth societies, the Vatican insisted upon a comprehensive and unequivocal agreement embracing all aspects of the problem—thus, a raising of the ban on dual membership should be a stipulated part of that overall agreement with the state and ought not to rest on mere assurances of party authorities. In that connection, the note continued, the Holy See had been alarmed by statements made by party members during the course of the talks that the concordat was binding upon the state but not upon the party, and wanted that matter cleared up. In order to reopen discussion on this and other points, the representatives of the Church would again resume contact with the representatives of the government.[7]

Negotiations were again under way on September 14, and the bishops submitted a new draft securing the incorporation bodily of the workers' associations into Catholic Action and reserving for the Catholic youth the right to wear distinctive clothing and to engage in pursuits "necessary to the health and joy of youth, which serve to train the young in discipline, (gymnastics, swimming, games, wandering, camping, and folk-dancing)"; competitive sports were surrendered to the state.[8] There was some desire in the foreign ministry to reach an agreement before the Saar plebiscite, but the negotiations ran aground on the question of youth organizations, and on the proposal of the Holy See to incorporate occupational associations bodily into Catholic Action. Hitler regarded both of the Church's conditions as unacceptable.[9] Consequently, on November 7, the government prepared another draft agreement, which Buttmann submitted to the bishops; on November 17, the nuncio in Berlin, Monsignor Orsenigo, informed the foreign ministry that the Vatican found the draft of November 7 only slightly better than the June draft which it had already rejected. The Reich government had planned to send Buttmann to Rome to continue discussions, but Monsignor Orsenigo expressed the opinion of the Vatican that such a journey at this time would be premature. Indeed, the Vatican wished to obtain clarification before Buttmann's departure of the points in dispute in order to prevent another vain journey which would simply complicate efforts. A few days later, when Neurath questioned the nuncio as to his powers to negotiate, Monsignor Orsenigo said that he had none, but merely hoped in conversations with Buttmann to promote definition of the two points of view, and possibly some reconciliation of them.

Apparently, Cardinal Pacelli intended neither to truncate negotiations, nor to deter Buttmann from proceeding to Rome; but rather to use as a threat with which to win concessions the statement that Buttmann's trip to the Vatican at present seemed futile. The tactic failed. Hitler had already decided not to send Buttmann to Rome.[10] and used the opportunity to prolong the negotiations; the foreign ministry later imputed the delays to the Vatican because of its unwillingness to receive Buttmann in November. Already, by November 29, Monsignor Orsenigo apparently realized the mistake and emphasized to Menshausen of the foreign ministry that he had in no way wished to obstruct Buttmann's visit, but on the contrary had been instructed to explain to Buttmann that his presence at the Vatican would lead to nothing if he could offer no sounder proposals than those submitted to the bishops on November 7. During this same discussion, the nuncio emphasized that a disavowal by Hitler of neo-heathenism was a requisite for any final settlement of the discords between Church and state; Menshausen countered that Hitler had promised such a statement when the negotiations had been satisfactorily completed. Early in December, Monsignor Orsenigo opened discussions with Buttmann that proceeded intermittently for some days thereafter.

On December 18, the foreign ministry sent a note to the Vatican explaining why it had never answered the cardinal secretary of state's notes of May 14 and September 2. The government had not replied to these notes, it said, because it considered it more expedient to settle existing differences by oral discussions; also, the Reich government had been prepared to send Buttmann to Rome, but at the suggestion of the Holy See, had agreed that Buttmann should enter into discussions with the nuncio.

Cardinal Pacelli had been temporarily out-maneuvered. The unfortunate draft agreement of June, and the Vatican's rejection of it, made it possible for the Reich government to blame the Holy See for the delay in arrival at a settlement; the nuncio's suggestion that Buttmann delay his departure made it possible for the Reich to accuse the Vatican of prolonging the negotiations; and as the German note again pointed out, the Führer's slated renunciation of neo-heathenism was contingent upon completion of talks. In sum, according to the Reich thesis, only the Church's intransigence, and its unwillingness to abide by the June draft stood in the way of a satisfactory adjustment.

Actually, the negotiations were a sham. Hitler intended to concede nothing. The discussions had served to avert a public denunciation by the Pope, or a rupture of relations, which might have adversely affected the Saar vote. However, after January 15, 1935, when the tally of the Saar plebiscite was completed, and the vote overwhelmingly for reunion with Germany, Hitler could ignore the wishes of the Vatican. In mid-December, Neurath had written to Frick concerning Orsenigo's desire for a statement against neo-heathenism by Hitler and had recommended that, in view of the political advantages of a settlement with the Church, such a statement ought to be considered. On January 26, the nuncio was again pressing Neurath for the statement, and the foreign minister drew up a memorandum on the matter for Hitler's attention. Hitler now flatly refused to make such a declaration. Then, on January 28, Buttmann met with Monsignor Orsenigo and Bishop Berning, and informed them that Hitler had decided to abide by the June draft and could make no further concessions.

On January 29, the Vatican presented Bergen with a note replying to the German note of December 18, 1934. The cardinal secretary of state pointed out that the Holy See did not oppose on principle the German preference for oral discussions rather than an exchange of diplomatic notes, but in practice, the direct discussions had not proved much superior to an exchange of notes. Apparently, the method of exchanging notes had been of little use, for Cardinal Pacelli then listed a long series of missives to the German government which had never received replies. The foreign ministry dared not dismiss this note as abruptly as Hitler could terminate oral negotiations; fearing the Vatican might publish a White Book, as it had often threatened to do, the Germans had to be ready with documents of their own to publish in turn and consequently, on April 16, 1935, the foreign ministry played another card in the diplomatic game with a note to answer Cardinal Pacelli's complaints. The German note argued that if oral mediation had failed to produce results it was the fault of the Church. In the first place, the government had thought that the bishops in June, 1934 were empowered to reach a concord, and the bishops had given no indication that that assumption was false; since no mention was made at the time of submitting the final document to the members of the hierarchy, and the bishops had assured the government that demurs were not to be expected, the government had assumed that approval would be a matter of form; finally, the rejection of the results by the Vatican had caused the delay in reaching an understanding. As for the unreciprocated notes cited by Cardinal Pacelli; they had either been answered in one form or another, or dealt with matters reserved for mutual discussions. The Government assured the cardinal that it hoped to deal with these unsettled matters either "in writing, or by means of oral negotiations", and that it looked forward to a settlement and therefore awaited "with particular interest the observations of His Excellency the Nuncio upon the communication made to him by *Ministerialdirektor* Dr. Buttmann at their most recent conversation on January 28 last." Since Buttmann's "communication" at that time had been to tell the nuncio that Hitler had decided to revert to the June draft and refused further concessions, the German position actually was that the government placed the blame on the Holy See for the breakdown of negotiations because it had disdained the June agreement, and that while Germany might resume talks, it assured the Vatican in advance that the Reich government would concede nothing. Cardinal Pacelli responded later with a note pointing out the speciousness of some of the German arguments, but by then the arena had shifted from the chancelleries, to the police offices and the streets.[11]

CHAPTER TEN

Tightening the Screws

Nazi strategy against the churches

Hitler and Schirach had been very successful in dealing with the Evangelical youth. There, they had been able to count upon the support of a large pro-Nazi faction within the Evangelical Church, the German Christians. Thus advantaged, Hitler had created a new office in the Evangelical Church, that of *Reichsbishop*, and elevated to it Ludwig Müller, a National Socialist. On his own authority, and against the wishes of the leader of the Evangelical Youth, Müller ceded their associations to the Hitler Youth.

Approaching the Catholic youth groups, Hitler had attempted to subvert them from the top as well, and obtain their surrender by the Pope. That ran aground because Pius XI was personally committed to the youth organizations and regarded them not only as a timely and indispensable method of Christian education, but also as the first defense against the "religion" of Blood and Soil permeating the Hitler Youth. Moreover, the will of the individual members to persevere proved difficult to shake. Hitler planned next to maneuver through the bishops, and the draft agreement which the German government won in June 1934 would have resolved the dilemma once and for all by remitting the claims of the Church; but the ultimate authority in such matters was the Pope, and his views remained unchanged. As long as he chose to preserve the youth associations, and as long as the individual members could not be dissuaded from adhering to those organizations, no triumph over intermediaries would solve the problem in favor of the Nazis. But now, with the Saar plebiscite over, negotiation could be dispensed with and the field of action transferred from the highest to the lowest level; instead of dealing with the Vatican, the Nazis could cope with the organizations and their membership with methods they knew best, bringing to bear upon them the full weight of the coercive faculties of the regime.

After January 1935 and the Saar plebiscite, the position of the churches in German society came increasingly under attack. Hitler

129

unleashed the head of the neo-heathen German Faith Movement, Jakob Wilhelm Hauer, who at the end of 1934 had been obliged to curtail his propaganda until after the Saar plebiscite. In February 1935 Hauer was given full rein and the movement began holding as many as sixty rallies a week. The cause, however, was so radical it aroused a storm of protest from the Evangelicals and the Catholics, and by June 1935 was already being disclaimed by important leaders in state and party. More significant in the long run, was the Nazi policy of strictly separating church and state, exemplified in a Hitler Youth decree of January 18, 1935, prohibiting HJ and *Jungvolk* from serving mass in uniform.[1] In Munich, a campaign was launched to persuade parents to opt for the interdenominational school, and when the students were signed up in February, instead of the usual 84 per cent, only 64 per cent were enrolled for confessional schools. School authorities everywhere began to "consult" parents, imposing myriad pressures to decide for the interdenominational (secular) school, as was the Führer's wish. People were pressed to sign petitions for fear of losing their livelihood, and election results were tampered with. By 1938, the number of Catholic confessional schools had been reduced almost by half;[2] early 1935 also saw the beginning of the systematic exclusion of clergy from giving religious instruction in confessional schools and the inception of the drive to eliminate private schools.

The campaign against organized Catholic youth now became part of this broader drive for the "deconfessionalization of public life," as Frick put it.[3] For the Nazis, driving the churches from public life was but to limit them to their proper sphere. As Hans Kerrl, appointed in July 1935 to head the new ministry of ecclesiastical affairs, stated in a speech the following October: "Religion has nothing to do with the practical realities of this life."[4]

During 1935, Catholic youth membership and groups began to meet with varied coercion. On November 30, 1934, Schirach had added another disability to not belonging to the Hitler Youth when the members of the gymnastic and sports associations were incorporated into the Hitler Youth.[5] That agreement shifted the focus of the Hitler Youth to some extent, leaving it much more sports-oriented and giving it a practical monopoly on competitive sports.

Catholic youth resist

The Catholic youth meanwhile was holding out, though it had suffered losses. Father Heinrich Roth, head of the JMV of the diocese of Münster, noted in October 1934, that the membership loss in his diocese had been 31 per cent, and losses of about one-third seemed to be fairly typical. Yet in some places, the groups had actually increased.[6] It was a curious phenomenon that despite (or due to) all of the pressures, Catholic youth groups should thrive, but one to recur in Essen in the spring of 1935, when impositions of Hitler Youth were at their worst. The occasion was a "spring offensive" conducted by the Hitler Youth from March 24 to April 7 in the Ruhr-Niederrhein region, with the object of convincing "the very last decent thinking German youth that he belongs in the HJ."[7] Schirach himself set the tone of the "offensive" with a speech in Essen on March 31, in which he examined the claim of the Catholic youth to have sports.

I ask you, my comrades, what has sports to do with confession? Have you ever seen a Catholic or Evangelical sport? Do you know what a Catholic revolution around a bar or an Evangelical pull-up is? Those are the excuses and subterfuges of those who are always against Germany. It is not a matter of religion, it is a matter of their posts: They assert that they serve religious education, but they serve no other God than their bellies.[8]

Other prominent leaders, including Reich and Prussian Minister of Education Bernhard Rust, came to the region as speakers; the press and radio stood at the service of the campaign, while in the schools, the teachers used their authority to recruit for the HJ. In the factories, party officials and employers pressed Catholic youth to join the Hitler Youth under threat of dismissal, and employment offices offered special advantages to *Hitlerjugend*; the Hitler Youth held assemblies in the schools and factories which all students and young workers were required to attend. Marching columns of Hitler Youth, bearing posters, went through the streets seeking out members of the Catholic groups and their parents to "persuade" them to come over to the Hitler Youth. Public officials whose children were in the Catholic youth were told that their oath to the Führer placed them under a moral obligation to send their children to the Hitler Youth.

The Catholic youth member was treated as an outlaw. During the offensive, the police station in Essen was decorated with a huge poster which bore the insignia of the police on one side, and that of the HJ on the other, and in great block letters shouted "The Police Stand By The Hitler Youth!" And so they did. The police arrived too late to prevent outrages upon the property and persons of Catholic youth and were unable to apprehend the perpetrators of those acts. When complaints were signed against Hitler Youth, the proceedings were usually dismissed as insignificant, or quashed on the ground that the Hitler Youth member would be punished by the HJ; while on the contrary, members of the Catholic youth who defended themselves were likely to be put in jail. When the alarm was raised in an attack in Essen-Altendorf, a *Hitlerjugend* shouted "Police stand with the HJ!" Thus, reports from other areas of Hitler Youth breaking into homes and stealing or destroying property were not to be wondered at.

In a speech reported from Leipzig on April 9, Schirach said, "It will be decided in the coming weeks whether the Catholics will possess enough sense to give up on their own accord this cliquish and disloyal system of theirs, or whether it will be necessary to use force ... And unless the devil himself is against us, we will succeed in compelling Catholics just as we've compelled the one hundred and one other clubs and associations."[9] Certainly the devil was not against him, but if we are to judge from the results in Essen, a good deal of force—sometimes of a novel sort—would have to be employed. The problem is illustrated graphically by this table prepared from Heinrich Roth, *Katholische Jugend in der NS-Zeit.*[10]

The so-called spring [1935] offensive of the HJ was most intensive in Essen. We give here the real effect of the "spring offensive" in Essen according to the most exact and reliable sources:

Effect in 53 parishes in Essen:

	Under 14 years	Over 14 years	Total
Left the Catholic Youth	*160*	*22*	*182*
to enter the Hitler Youth	*124*	*17*	*141*
Newly entering the Catholic Youth	*407*	*637*	*1044*
coming from the HJ	*29*	*29*	*58*
Net increase for the Catholic Youth:	*862*		

The question which jumps out from these figures is why such a large group of previously uncommitted young people suddenly decided to put themselves in jeopardy and join the Catholic youth groups.

It should be stated at the outset that Essen may have been a special case. The great demonstration of Essen-Werden on June 28, 1934 brought out as many unorganized as organized Catholic youth;[11] there may have been a special relationship between the organized and unorganized youth which did not prevail elsewhere. On the other hand, it may not have been so much the Catholic organizations which determined the figures, as something about the Church proper; perhaps they reflect a precedented reaction to persecution. Yet if that were true, it would be hard to account for the losses of approximately one-third which the JMV had experienced since the rise of the Nazi regime. I would suggest that part of the explanation for the sudden Catholics' fervor may lie in the suddenness and concentration of Nazi harassment. It could be that the Catholic youth and the Hitler Youth had divided and confused the consciences of young Catholics who were torn between loyalty to their faith and allegiance to the Fatherland. Nazi accusations were aimed at making the religious person equate "confessionalism" with diverse particularism and disloyalty to the state. No doubt, some Catholics suffered guilt over the matter. Thus, a corollary inference would be that the uncommitted group of young Catholics had a special awareness of the conflict, and an especially acute ambivalence toward the conflicting value systems with which they were presented. It is certain, at least, that they were formally committed to neither side. While possibly feeling remiss about not belonging to the Hitler Youth, had they joined the HJ, their encounter with its ideology, and the resultant jarring of their Christian values would have caused them to feel even less justified; therefore, they remained formally neutral. But when the HJ chose a frontal assult, the Nazi youth bloc ceased to represent a virtue—loyalty to the Fatherland—and instead came to embody a clear evil: savage external aggression aimed at destroying Church entities and perhaps the Church itself. By turning objective and menacing, the HJ and the values it represented may have ceased to operate internally to produce moral quandary in the Catholic youth; with the Nazis' emergence as extrinsic foe, the conscience was freed, and the "neutralized" young person could at last embrace with certitude the formations and symbols of his, or her faith.   The decision itself was certainly an heroic one, and a manifest anomaly in a system whose chief feature was to make opportunists of nearly everyone. The history of this period, so dark in most respects, is brightened by this example.

Another fact which stands out from the figures, is that the older organized Catholic youth were practically invulnerable to the pressures and persuasions of the HJ.   Yet, despite the magnificent display of courage by its adherents old and new, the JMV had little cause to rejoice.   An indication that while Nazi youth had obviously lost the battle of Essen, it may have been winning the war was that although the Catholic youth groups of Essen had lost only 17 members over the age of fourteen to the Hitler Youth, they had lost 124 under fourteen.   If that was due to the fact that *Jungschar* members had not had time to develop the binding sense of community that was a source of strength to the older age groups, that would be serious enough, but if the relative weakness of the younger members was due to the fact that more of their formative years had been spent under Nazi indoctrination in the schools, then that was even more insidious in the long run for the religious youth and for the Church itself.   Certainly, there was something different about this age group; notice the figures of the uncommitted who entered the Catholic youth: 407 under the age of fourteen entered, while over the age of fourteen the figure was a third higher: 637.   Those uncommitted in either age group were not likely to respond primarily to communal spirit in making decisions, so apparently, the difference in age, or something connected with the difference in age, was a crucial determining factor.

Whatever the factor was, whether it had something to do with informal connections with Catholic youth organizations, with Nazi indoctrination or pressure at the earlier school years, or with the psychology of the different age levels, the disparity in behavior in the groups apparently was not lost on Schirach.   At the beginning of 1936, he launched a massive campaign throughout Germany to enroll every 10 year old boy and girl in the *Jungvolk* and BDM on April 19, the eve of Hitler's birthday.   Recruiting offices were set up, and the HJ carried on an enormous campaign of pressure and propaganda. The Reich minister of education had prohibited school flags and class pennants on July 22, 1935; now on March 11, 1936, schools were permitted to fly the HJ flag provided 90 per cent of the students belonged to the Hitler Youth, which must have put intolerable pressure on the remaining hold-outs. The campaign was entirely successful and enrolled nearly every able-bodied ten year old in the country.[12] The campaign extended from the eleven to fourteen year olds and by June nearly all of the age group 10-14 had been enrolled in the *Jungvolk*.[13] Yet, that time only 70-80 per cent of the older youth were in the Hitler Youth.[14] The surprising fact about those figures when compared with those of the "spring offensive", is that they suggest that the influence of parents was in no way decisive. Surely, the parents who wanted their children aged 14-18 to stay out of the Hitler Youth wanted their children aged 10-14 to remain out as well. Yet those children were unable to resist joining the *Jungvolk* regardless of how their parents felt. The younger group could have been the Achilles heel of the Catholic youth organizations, but Schirach and the police were not patient enough to let them die of attrition, and the Nazi regime had the power to destroy them directly.

Not that the Catholic youth were totally defenseless. A *Sicherheitsdienst* report from Koblenz, prepared in April, 1935,[15] showed that the youth groups had factors working in their favor too, although they in no way matched the sinister assets of the Hitler Youth. Some teachers in the Koblenz region assigned the theme "Why am I not in the *Jungvolk*?". The clergy or Catholic lay forces apparently had a hand in preparing this assignment, for from nine different localities approximately 160 assignments came in, most bearing the argument: "I am in the *Jungschar*. Here I have a strong loyalty, and a German youth does not break his oath. My parents will not tolerate my entering the *Jungvolk*." Apparently, some Hitler Youth members retained membership in the Catholic Youth despite Schirach's decree against double membership, and they were encouraged in that by the Catholics who urged them "not to break the vow given to Christ." The latter carried on an effective propaganda through handbills and circular letters, and priests threw themselves into the struggle. From the pulpit, they reminded parents that some day they would be held accountable for the souls of their children. Priests went out on personal visits to parents to persuade them to keep their children in the Catholic youth affiliations. When a family received aid from the Catholic charity organization *Caritas*, it ran the risk of losing that assistance if the child moved to the Nazi side. The *Neudeutschen, Werkjugend,* and JMV continued to exist as separate organizations, but at the local level they stood firmly behind the leadership of a clergyman to form a united Catholic youth bloc.

The *Sicherheitsdienst* report shows that in the Koblenz region Catholic youth groups, with the exception of *Neudeutschland,* were doing very well. A newly founded JMV group in Mengershausen had a membership of 35 a few days after its establishment. Another group was founded in Meudt and twenty boys entered. In Offenbach, the "black corner," the JMV was very active, and its propaganda quite effective. The Catholic youth of the Koblenz region were notably bold, and despite the prohibition against wearing uniforms, members were sometimes seen on the street in full regalia; should a *Hitlerjugend* make a remark, there might be a fight.

An advantage which the Catholic youth apparently enjoyed, which may have offset slightly the many employment difficulties, was an alleged preference given to their entering the *Reichswehr.* The national leadership of the JMV in Düsseldorf was supposed to have very good connections with the *Reichswehr* service offices. Approximately a fifth of the *Reichswehr* officers in 1932 were Catholic when the army numbered only 100,000, and since that time many of them had been promoted to higher offices. They reportedly retained contact with their former *Präses* and accepted their recommendations for new recruits. The SD had evidence of a case where members of the *Sturmschar* were taken into the *Reichswehr* on the recommendation of their priest, while a member of the HJ from the same locality was rejected. The *Ortsgruppe* of the NSDAP informed the *Reichswehr* service offices of the "national unreliability of the *Sturmschar* members," but nothing happened. On the contrary, there were indications that the letters from the *Ortsgruppe* were made available to the *Sturmschar.*

The Catholic youth may have had a rudimentary intelligence system. The SD uncovered evidence of one attempt to have a Catholic youth member enter the HJ for the purpose of spying, and the police were aware that the Catholic youth were extremely well-informed about what took place in the Hitler Youth.

The Catholic bodies benefited from the clash of allegiances, and even *Ortsgruppenleiter* were known to intercede for the Catholic youth and let the HJ and BDM decline.[16] And decline they did, in some regions. A report from the Hitler Youth *Bannführer* of Recklinghausen of January 17, 1935 complained that in the month of December 1934, 900 members had dropped out of the HJ. The reason, as far as he knew, was the incompetence of the subordinate leaders, who did not know even how to arrange and sustain an evening's program.[17] Desperation such as that at Recklinghausen may have promoted the efforts of Hitler Youth to destroy competing organizations. It apparently was easier to enroll HJ than to keep them enrolled.

The *Bannführer's* report from Recklinghausen may have fallen into the hands of the Catholic youth, which would account for its appearance in Heinrich Roth's *Katholische Jugend in der NS-Zeit.* Roth published another document which Monsignor Wolker incorporated into a report to the episcopate of November, 1935. The document, a letter dated August 8, 1935 from the *Standortsführer* to the *Banne* and *Jungbanne* in his area, must have reached the Catholic youth from someone in the HJ. The *Standortsführer* had obtained a list of all of the secondary school students in Essen who belonged to Catholic youth groups, along with their fathers' occupations and places of employment. In one gymnasium, he discovered that over 120 youth were still active in the Catholic youth organizations, and that 36 of those were sons of government employees. He recommended that every school be investigated in this way, and copies of the results sent to the school authorities, the National Socialist Teachers' League, and to the NSDAP offices.[18]

Applying coercion to civil servants to send their children into the HJ was officially adopted at the Reich level, by an order issued by the Führer's Deputy Rudolf Hess, on August 24, 1935.

The Führer has given to the party the task of educating all German men to National Socialist thought and behavior in the service of the German Volk. In the realm of this task, the Hitler Youth alone (which as the organization of the party which bears the name of the Führer) according to his will is called to lead German boys and girls in behavior and life outlook, in a National Socialist way, and to prepare them physically and mentally for their own task as bearers of the Reich.

It is, therefore, self-evident that anyone who takes honorably his confession to the Führer and his movement, out of responsible consciousness of the German future, will clear the way for his children to enter the Hitler Youth and thus support the work of the Führer.

This readiness, which I assume on the part of party members and members of the organizations, I believe especially may be expected in the case of any who as officials and sworn servants of the National Socialist state must regard it as their first and highest duty to pledge their strength, and their lives for the existence and the preservation of the Reich. Whoever wishes to serve the Führer ought to do nothing which opposes his duty to Volk and Führer. The Reich will not be saved through supineness and lukewarm compromises.

In this connection, I turn quite clearly against the conception put forth from many sides that it is unnecessary to enter the Hitler Youth since, for example, belonging to a purely religious youth group recognized by the state substitutes for the Hitler Youth. This view is just as erroneous as if someone were to assert that he had gone to church and thereby had fulfilled his duty with regard to Volk and Reich. . . . Anyone who by any insinuation whatsoever denies his children the membership in the Hitler Youth which they desire, acts in an irresponsible manner and is to be regarded as an opponent of the National Socialist state and its Führer.

Signed: R. Hess[19]

Repressive measures

Whatever the factors working for the Catholic youth, they were slight indeed compared to the arbitrary means available to the regime. This was amply illustrated late in April 1935, shortly after the "spring offensive," when members of the *Neudeutschland Bund, St. Georgs Pfadfinderschaft,* and *Strumschar* returned from an Easter pilgrimage to Rome. They had met with complete courtesy from the Italian and Swiss custom guards, but the German border was another matter. The sixty buses with 1700 pilgrims were stopped at the customs office, and SS and Gestapo officials detained them well into the night. The police confiscated 70,000 RM in property from them including uniforms, knapsacks, canteens, tents, musical instruments, suitcases, photographs, cameras, and binoculars. Even prayer books, rosaries, souvenirs, and devotional momentos were taken. The treatment of persons was in the fashion of the police state, insulting and without regard for personal rights. The young men were breaking no law, there was no prohibition against wearing uniforms for the Reich as a whole, and in Baden, where the incident occurred, the wearing of uniforms was still permitted. The Pope, of course, was deeply outraged and expressed to the next band of German pilgrims the hope that they would be better treated than the last.[20]

The beginning of the end for the Catholic youth groups came in July, 1935. In a message to district officials on July 8 Goering set the tone.

"[The Church] cannot call upon God against this state, a monstrosity which we experience every Sunday in open or concealed ways, nor can it be permitted to organize its own political power under the pretext that it must parry threatening dangers from the state. It has applied those abbreviations which have entered into the flesh and blood of all Germans, like HJ (*Hitlerjugend*) to the Heart of Jesus, (*Herz Jesu*); BDM (*Bund Deutscher Mädel*) to League of Daughters of Mary, (*Bund der Marienmädchen*); and applied the German Greeting (*Deutscher Grüss*) to Jesus Christ."[21]

On July 16, Goering issued a decree against "political Catholicism" in which he threatened with suppression Catholic youth formations that engaged in anything other than strictly religious activities. On July 23, he issued a police order for Prussia on the matter. Such groups were forbidden practices not of a purely religious sort, and particularly any incursions into the political or sports realms. Wearing of uniforms, or of uniform clothing, or even of insignia was banned, even if worn under other clothes. Wandering, tent camps, and closed column marching were prohibited, and so was the making of music.

Bearing of banners except as occasioned by traditional processions and pilgrimages, and at funerals and church celebrations, was also prohibited; violators could be punished with fines or incarceration. By September, this decree had been applied to the entire Reich.[22]

The same day that Goering's decree was issued in Prussia, in Baden the minister of interior dissolved the DJK and confiscated its goods; the youth organizations there were denied any activity. The pretext was an incident in the town of Weiher, where a local subordinate leader of the HJ complained that he had been assaulted by eight to ten members of the DJK and knocked unconscious; the Catholic investigation of the charge indicated it was more likely that the *Hitlerjugend* had been drinking and fell from his bicycle. In August, the Baden secret police dropped the case for lack of evidence, and while the DJK in Baden remained dissolved, had to lift suppression of activities for the rest of Catholic youth there.[23]

Goering's prohibition was assiduously enforced. In Viersen on August 17, six Catholic youth picked up for wandering were fined 150 RM each, or a total of 900 RM, and ten members of the local JMV were fined a total of 1050 RM for marching in a column and wearing similar clothing; an official of the Labor Front then had the flagrant offenders fired from their jobs as "enemies of the state." A newspaper account of the trial made the lesson explicit: "Parents, be warned."

Meanwhile, action was taken against leaders. A decree of August 15 issued by the Reich Ministry of Churches prohibited anyone giving religious instruction in the higher schools from also providing·spiritual care for a confessional youth youngster.[24]

The bishops assembled in plenary conference at Fulda on August 20 prepared a pastoral letter calling upon young Catholics to stay firm in the faith, to maintain self-discipline and not meet force with force, and to obey the laws against public appearances and uniform clothing until those laws were changed.[25] That same day, a memorandum submitted by all of the Catholic groups to the conference at Fulda revealed a deep sense of betrayal. The organizations assured the bishops of their loyalty to the state and asked them to make their support for Catholic organizations both public and unequivocal. Too often their lot had been "martyrdom without mandate," they complained, because highly placed ecclesiastics minimized the importance of the organizations, regarded them as dispensable, or dismissed the suppression of a group or the arrest of a leader as warranted by an overdaring policy. The bishops replied with a special letter of commitment to the organizations telling them that they participated with heavy heart in the sufferings and sacrifices made by so many members and leaders. Just as they had not forsaken their bishops, neither would the bishops abandon them, but would do everything they could to secure their rights. As with the pastoral, there was a note of moderation and caution in this reply. The bishops welcomed the assurances of the groups that they were in no way hostile to the state and had no political connections, especially with the communists, and were therefore entitled to the protection of the concordat.[26]

The theme of communist ties to Catholic youth had been exploited by Nazi propaganda during the summer of 1935 and became a fertile theme for the police to pursue. Apparently, there was a modicum of truth in it. *Jungführer* took the results of the subsequent trials of youth leaders seriously enough to disavow Catholic leaders convicted of having had contacts with communists, and called upon the Catholic youth to report to the police approaches made by communists. But there was far more smoke than fire, and the police used the charge to arrest many youth leaders who were later released or acquitted.

Systematic repressive actions against the JMV and its leaders began on November 19, 1935 with the closing of the *Jugendhaus* in Düsseldorf by the secret police in concert with the ministry of ecclesiastical affairs. In a letter of November 22, Monsignor Wolker assured his reader that the offices had been occupied for purposes of investigation, not confiscation. Despite the false rumors, the Monsignor added, no one had been arrested. He ought to have added "as yet," for on the following day, General Secretary Clemens was arrested and taken to Berlin. On February 5, Franz Steber, former Reich leader of the *Sturmschar,* was arrested, and on February 6, Wolker himself. On February 21, newspapers announced the arrests of seven communist leaders, ten priests, and forty-five lay officials of the JMV by the Gestapo in the Rhineland and Westphalia. Among those arrested was Hans Niermann, present Reich leader of the *Sturmschar.* On December 5, 1935, the Gestapo had released some of the rooms of the *Jugendhaus,* but still invested all of those necessary for official business. Finally, on May 12, 1936, the Gestapo restored the remaining rooms and at that same time freed Monsignor Wolker. General Secretary Clemens continued in custody, although his health required his transfer to a sanatorium in July. On November 6, 1936, Hans Niermann was released. Finally, Clemens, Steber, and others were judged by the People's Tribunal in Berlin on April 28, 1937. Clemens and two others were acquitted. Steber was punished with five years imprisonment, and five years loss of civil rights; one defendant was sentenced to 11 years imprisonment; another to two years; and the last to 18 months, fourteen of which he had already served. The police also harassed the JMV to prevent its holding a Reich meeting. The organization had announced a projected Reich meeting as early as February 6, 1935. It had to postpone the meeting twice during the course of the year and finally set the date for October 31 to November 3. On October 25, the JMV had to send out telegrams calling off the scheduled meeting because it could not satisfy recently presented police demands concerning the meeting in the time remaining.

One of the critical blows to the JMV was a decree of January 11, 1936 by the president of the Reich Press Chamber, excluding from that body the press which published *Michael,* and the other Catholic youth literature. *Michael* (formerly *Junge Front*), the key target of the decree, with a circulation of nearly 300,000 was one of the financial mainstays of the organization; and since the leadership organs (*Jungführer, Jugendpräses*) were also affected by the order, the work of the JMV was nearly paralyzed. Protests by Cardinals Schulte and Bertram, and Bishops Berning and Galen were to no avail, and the president of the Reich Press Chamber held to his decision, pointing out that *Michael* had proved itself unable to put itself at the service of the "*Volk* movement."[27] *Michael* had managed to sustain an independent editorial policy, which had earned a number of prohibitions and confiscations; as recently as December 1, 1935, an issue had been confiscated. On May 1, 1936, the other publications of the JMV were allowed to reappear, but not *Michael.* To help offset the loss, the organization launched a drive in November and the following months to increase subscriptions to *Am Scheideweg* and in

April and May 1937, launched a campaign to increase the subscriptions to *Die Wacht.*[28]

The liquidation of *Michael* may not have been intended primarily as a direct blow against the youth organizations. Since April, 1935, the Reich Press Chamber had been effectively bringing the whole of the German press under Nazi control, and the *Michael* action may have been no more than a step in this campaign. The Nazi regime could mount crusades from as many directions as there were agencies aspiring to recast their assigned spheres. This case illustrates again the unique power base and resiliency of the Catholic Church, a supranational entity distinct from any party or nation, wholly vulnerable in all its members yet integral despite mutilation. Not only was the seat of Catholic authority far removed from Germany's borders, it comprised itself a state. *Michael,* to the last uncontaminated by the "*Volk* movement," was suppressed, but avoided a worse fate. The Catholic Church, as a true international organization, could not become involved in any nation's "*Volk* movement," especially when that movement was racist. The Papacy, the ultimate judge of all Church policies, even aside from its spiritual tasks, could never be at once international, and Aryan racist.

CHAPTER ELEVEN

The End of the JMV

The state youth

Schirach intended to evolve a state youth organization to which all German children would belong. He began with the youngest, planning to use draconian means, if necessary, to enroll the entire age group 10-14, but seeking first to enroll the children "voluntarily," that is, without legal compulsion. He proclaimed 1936 the "Year of German *Jungvolk*" and launched a ponderous campaign to induct all of the ten year olds on April 19, the eve of Hitler's birthday. The campaign was wholly successful with the ten year olds, and in April, it was also apparent that by June nearly all of the 11-14-year-old group would be devoured as well.

Schirach was now ready to unfold his plans. He prepared a draft law which set up a Reich youth organization to develop the moral and physical faculties of the whole German youth and to educate it in the spirit of National Socialism.[1] A new office was provided for, Youth Leader of the German Reich, its holder to be responsible directly to Hitler. Schirach sent the draft and a memorandum explaining the project to Rudolf Hess, the Führer's deputy. Hess passed these documents on to Robert Ley, who, besides heading the Labor Front, served as Organization Leader of the NSDAP.

The memorandum pointed out that since the age group 10-14 would soon be assimilated *in toto* into the *Jungvolk*, the compulsory aspect of the law would apply in practice only to the juveniles aged 14-18 who, upon completion of their service in the *Jungvolk*, were not selected to serve in the HJ. Those young people would be inducted into a proposed organization called the *Deutsche Jungmannschaft,* whose leaders would wear the uniform of the HJ, but whose members would wear a different uniform. The Youth Leader of the German Reich was to oversee the physical training of the whole of German youth according to the guidelines of the Reich war minister,

145

and the ideological guidance of the *Deutsche Jungmannschaft* in accordance with the thought of the Third Reich.

Since means were not at hand to set up the Reich youth organization until 1938 or early 1939, implementation up to that time would be preparatory. Hoping to draw talent from all of the Nazi organizations to fill key positions in the Reich youth administration, Schirach also indicated he was looking forward to an eventual unification under one official aegis of all matters concerning youth, the responsibility for which at present was scattered through the different ministries. He asked the party leaders not only to focus on the median objective of establishing a Reich youth organization, but also to think in terms of an elemental re-ordering of state youth work.

After a series of conferences with Schirach, Ley consented to the founding of an official Reich youth, provided that its direction lay undivided in the hands of the Hitler Youth. He hoped thereby to confirm the influence of the party over the new organization and preclude the possibility of raising a rival to the HJ.[2] The net effect of Ley's suggestion was to ensure Schirach's further aggrandizement. The latter had modestly left blank the space provided for the name of the Youth Leader in his draft law, but Ley's recommendation meant that the leader of the Hitler Youth was the logical man to lead the Reich youth.

Schirach had to abandon the clear distinction he wished to make between the party youth and the state youth: the Hitler Youth Law of December 1, 1936, an adapted version of Schirach's earlier draft, merged the "whole German Youth . . . into the Hitler Youth." With the first executive orders to the law issued in March, April, and November 1939, the Youth Leader was accorded full responsibility for German youth outside of home and school; HJ service was made compulsory for all children between the ages of ten and eighteen; parents were obligated to register their children for service; and each year, the new crop of 10-year-olds was inducted into the *Jungvolk* on the eve of Hitler's birthday. Although Schirach was unable to realize his plan for a *Jungmannschaft* organization of conscripts, distinct from the Hitler Youth, he attempted to differentiate between the new entries and the old—those enrolled before April 1939 were called *Stamm*

HJ; after one year, the new entry could aspire to *Stamm* HJ status as well—but in practice, the distinction proved negligible.[3]

The transformation of the HJ into a compulsory universal state youth organization was accompanied by the elaboration of disciplinary rules and regulations which proliferated into a thick book. Enforcement was carried out by the HJ Patrol Service, and by the youth superorganization's own special courts. By an agreement of October 7, 1938 between Schirach and Himmler, minions of the Patrol Service were looked upon as potential recruits for the SS and police, and the HJ took care to admit to the Service only those who met the racial and other prerequisites for admission into the SS. This was just one of the many ties linking the HJ to party and state. The youth organization had long been integrated with the party administration by a system which introduced Hitler Youth interns at every level; special naval, motor, flyer, and communications formations within the HJ prepared the young for the military services. The Hitler youth had evolved from the SA for adolescents which it once had been, into a vastly ramified and important element in the Nazi system.

The changing emphasis in Catholic youth work

Although the Hitler Youth Law of December 1, 1936 did not mean the immediate end of the Catholic youth organizations, it did reveal the rising momentum of the drive against them. Even before promulgation of the law, the Catholic Church had begun to lay preparations against the day when its extra-churchly youth organizations would formally cease to exist. A renewed emphasis upon religious celebrations, which had its origins in the spring of 1934 when the motive was not "purely religious," continued to manifest itself. At the Feast of Christ the King in October 1934, memorable celebrations involving the youth were held in the cathedrals at Aachen, Paderborn, Fulda, Augsburg, Münster, and Cologne. Cardinal Schulte was deeply moved by the celebration in his cathedral. Shortly before Christmas, he received the diocesan *Präses* in a special audience and thanked him for his work during that trying year. He spoke of his satisfaction with the observation of the Feast of Christ the King, in his cathedral, an experience which he said he would never forget. He had been so impressed, he prepared a special detailed report on the events of the Feast for the Pope.

January 1936 began the awesome campaign to enroll German youth into the *Jungvolk*. At the same time, anti-Christian propaganda was stepped up within the HJ. To deal with the youth problem, in January the bishops met in a special conference at Fulda. They decided to protest to the ministry of ecclestical affairs against the anti-Christian attitude of leaders of the HJ. The conference also took preliminary steps toward the creation of a new form of Catholic youth work.

The Fulda conferences of August, 1935 and of January, 1936 gave to Bishop Bornewasser of Trier the task of charting guidelines for the care of young souls. The episcopate was providing for the day when the fructive experiences of Catholic youth groups would have been brought to an end by the state, and the Church would have to vitalize youth work by other means. In line with this need, in February 1936, a meeting was held in Cologne of representatives of the six Church provinces and of the youth groups and the clerical head of the episcopal office for Catholic Action Peter Heuser. The conference discussed the proposals already thought out by Bishop Bornewasser and attempted to project a plan of youth work within the context of Catholic Action. The conference tried not to confine itself to consideration of youth in its present milieux but rather to think in broader terms and to keep in mind a binding of the "natural *and* supernatural, soul *and* body, activity of the priest *and* active cooperation of youth." The conference stressed the need of a nuclear body (*Kernschar*) for youth work and saw it at hand in the extant groups. The conferees requested that the bishops adopt and make obligatory for all priests a set of guidelines for the spiritual care of youth (*Jugendseelsorge*), erect an organ within the central committee of Catholic Action for the carrying through of those guidelines, and prepare a pastoral letter to the youth and their parents on the question of spiritual care for youth.[4]

The Guidelines were issued during the month of April. A letter elaborating upon the guidelines, prepared for publication in the various diocesan newspapers, revealed how much the Church had gleaned from the Catholic youth movement and its determination despite the times to uphold that heritage.[5] The letter stated that the guidelines were based upon the encyclical *Divini illius magistri*, issued by Pius

XI on December 31, 1929, which stressed the necessity of a youth work relevant beyond the formal confines of the Church. The fact that such a growth must suffer grave constriction at the moment did not mean that the Catholic Church renounced the extrachurchly realm. "For youth, religion cannot merely be a lifting of the heart on Sunday."

> *Educationally, a solely inner-churchly activity of the Catholic youth is always an imperfect piece of work (Stückwerk). . . . Christian youth need . . . homes, light, air, and the youthful joy of life. . . . Youth education and youth movement in the sense of the Church must have for its chief goal a development, leading, and care of religious life. . . . Not knowledge of articles of faith and prayers, but everyday life based on faith is the final goal of all proclamations of faith on Sunday and in solemn hours. Religious youth work therefore aims at the development of all God-given powers and talents. Only then can the Christian personality fulfill its life tasks in individual as well as in community life, especially in family, occupation, and Volk. Therefore, the different communities based on sex, stage of life, occupation, and so forth are to be furthered and are to shape their own forms of community life. . . .*

The letter pointed out that the *Kernscharen* referred to in the guidelines meant above all the existing youth groups, such as the JMV, *Jungfrauenverband, Kolpingsfamilie, Neudeutschland,* sodalities, and so forth. While the relation of the members to their extant organizations was not to be altered, the nucleus they comprised would be central to the new tasks of youth care. Special pains had to be taken in the selection of priests for the new work; for the most part, they would be drawn from those experienced in the spiritual ministry to the young, ready to cooperate with boy and girl youth leaders and to solicit the aid of the laity both in planning and execution. A responsible raising of young people to leadership capabilities was enjoined by the guidelines and was to be taken seriously; experienced workers knew how important that was.

The request of the Cologne conference for a statement concerning the spiritual care of youth was met on May 10, 1936 by a special pastoral letter from the episcopate to all young Catholics and their parents, giving them guidance for their behavior with regard to the Hitler Youth.[6] The letter said that those who attacked the Pope were the enemies of God, for they attacked the visible head of His Church. If the young person was brought into a movement or a *Bund* where God, religion, and the Church were not spoken of in the proper way, it was all the more imperative for him to turn to the Source of the Redeemer and defend himself against religious laxity. Should his Catholic faith be threatened by such a group, his obligation was to abjure that group, yet if such a crisis did not obtain, it was still his holy duty despite all attacks to be conscientiously Catholic; anyone who let a token Christianity suffice and severed himself from the community life of the parish youth, excusing himself with adversion to the attitude of the youth organization to which he belonged, thereby indicted that very organization. For where the bonds to God were thrown off other bonds were lacking as well. The "life nerve of the Catholic groups" was the "binding to God of the whole of youth life", the irradiation of the whole realm of act and omission, work and relaxation, occupation and joy, with the light of the holy faith."

> *The Church knows what it had and still has in its groups, the nuclear troop (Kernschar) of the Catholic youth. It secured for them the legal protection of the concordat. It watches over them like the apple of its eye. And the German bishops repeat today unanimously what the Holy Father proclaimed two years ago in his Easter message: "Your cause is our cause!" Yes, your cause is the cause of the Church of Christ; for it, for Christ, have they often treated you with mockery and derision, insulted your German honor and reproached you with un-German conduct. Many of you have sacrificed your goods, your future, your studies, your attendance at a university, yes many among you have put at stake freedom and life, truly, not for any group or pastime, but true to your motto "For the Kingdom of Christ in the new Germany!"*

Early in May, the bishop of Trier proposed a step which was to become a hallmark of Catholic youth work, a nationwide confession of faith by the whole Catholic youth to take place on Trinity Sunday, June 7.[7] On June 5, the Gestapo, which had learned that plans for the celebrations involved public appearances, invoked the decree of December 7, 1934 to insure that the event was purely sacred and prohibited any assembly outside of church grounds.[8] In Munich, Cardinal Faulhaber was met with an order to cancel his procession, but held it in defiance of the order.[9]

Another feature of the renewed scope of Catholic youth works was initiated in May 1936 with the inception of leadership training courses for young men. By the fall of 1936, 800 young men had already participated in the courses. The response to a course for priests engaged in youth work scheduled for October 7-12, 1937 was so avid that the number of participants from each diocese had to be limited; one hundred and five priests came for the course, and most stayed the full eight days. They were informed that the guidelines issued in April 1936 had been well-received in all dioceses by the priests and by the young; the establishment of episcopal offices for the spiritual succor of youth had been carried out in many dioceses, and execution of youth work according to the guidelines was under way. It was stressed that since the effort would rise or fall with the quality of leadership that endued it, the basic priorities were to interest the whole clergy in the new effort and to train both those entrusted with youth and their lay assistants. Accordingly, each trainee at the course was asked to begin to attend to these needs upon his return home. After careful groundwork, the bishops should call conferences to win over the clergy to the new effort and establish courses for training both priests who worked with youth and their young helpers.

It was none too soon. The terminal suppression of the JMV had already begun.

The end of the JMV

On July 27, 1937 the Gestapo dissolved the JMV within the diocese of Paderborn and confiscated its goods. The JMV had "repeatedly violated the order of July 23, 1935 against activities of the confessional youth groups by wanderings, tent camps, and games of sport." Any attempt to evade the order of dissolution was to be punished with not less than one month in jail or a fine of 150 to 15,000 RM. On October 27, the diocesan JMV of Münster was dissolved on the same grounds. The diocese of Trier met the same fate on November 12.

A meeting of the *Generalpräsidium* and *Reichsvorstand* of the JMV was called for November 19 to deal with the emergency created by the dissolutions of diocesan groups of Paderborn, Münster, Trier, and now on the day of the meeting, in a part of the archdiocese of Breslau. Meanwhile, the bishop of Mainz, at the urging of the two bishops of Trier, and after writing to Cardinal Bertram, had arranged for a meeting of the representatives of the bishops to be held in Frankfort on November 16 to consider what was to be done about the *Jugendhaus Düsseldorf*, e.V., the registered *Verein (eingetragener Verein)*, which held the property of the JMV. Since the problems of the two conferences were cognate, and since many of the delegates to one were also delegates to the other, both were brought to Cologne.[10]

The bishop of Mainz served as chairman of the meeting of diocesan representatives and opened with the question whether the episcopate should take the initiative and dissolve the JMV or wait for the police to do it. The question had great immediacy, for the diocese of Fulda planned to dissolve its diocesan group.

Monsignor Wolker presented the arguments for and against voluntary dissolution. Speaking first for voluntary dissolution, he presented the argument that it might be possible thereby to save some property of the JMV for other purposes, thus facilitating continued spiritual care for youth in accordance with the guidelines; part of the pastoral clergy was fatigued and skeptical, and a voluntary dissolution would lightened their load and leave a new basis of perseverence. Moreover, there was the question whether the organization membership had the economic, communal, and spiritual endurance to survive the destruction of the diocesan groups one by one.

Then, presenting the case against voluntary dissolution, Monsignor Wolker began with the legal consideration that since it involved a point of Church law fixed by the concordat, it was up to the Pope to decide. Second, dissolution could be considered only if it were accompanied by a strong unanimous statement from all pulpits, and the consequences of that course had to be thought through. Third, a defeat in this area might have a serious effect upon church life in general; giving up one point of the concordat might lead to action against other church groups. In closing, the monsignor stressed that a voluntary dissolution ought not to be contemplated unless there was clear recognition of the requisite steps to be taken in each diocese for a renewed care of youth.

After Monsignor Wolker's statement, the bishop of Mainz called upon the representatives of various dioceses for their opinions. The representatives from Breslau reported that Cardinal Bertram would not agree to a dissolution and that in the cardinal's opinion the episcopate did not have the prerogative to surrender anything. The representative from Cologne considered dissolution impossible on the grounds that the decision was up to the Pope. The representative from Fulda favored dissolution in order to salvage the resources to carry out work in line with the episcopal guidelines. The representative from Osnabrück had no special instructions from his bishop, but expressed an opinion he had often expressed before: future developments in the spiritual care of youth ought to follow the lines of Catholic Action according to the Osnabrück model. The representative from Freiburg echoed the opinion of Archbishop Gröber that the episcopate had no legal right to dissolve the organization and conveyed the archbishop's proposal that the conference ask the episcopate for a pastoral on the youth question. The representatives from Würzburg and Aachen both spoke against dissolution. The representative from Rottenburg announced the determination of his bishop to yield only to force and to maintain any group which had as many as three members. The representative from Munich had no special instructions in the matter, but observed that voluntary dissolution or no, the financial position of the group in Munich was becoming untenable.

Next, the bishop of Mainz raised the problem of what to do about the property of the JMV in Düsseldorf in order to protect it from confiscation. Monsignor Wolker and the legal counsel of the JMV advised that the property could not yet be transferred to the diocese of Cologne because it was liable for a still undetermined amount of taxes.[11] Castle Matgendorf, whose confessional school had been closed by the police, could be sold to the army administration, or that failing, allowed to revert to the state of Prussia which held the loan on it. *Haus Altenberg* was on the property of the archiepiscopal diocese of Cologne; the JMV, which had built the building, could give up its lease and transfer its rights to the archiepiscopal See. The latter should see to it that the house was reserved for the religious care of youth.

As for related exigencies, the refund of dues was left up to the dissolved diocesan groups; where their financial position was particularly shaken, a special arrangement might be reached. The accident insurance which had been carried on the members of the JMV would be allowed to lapse at the beginning of the new year in order to save the premium; in certain cases the diocesan group would provide assistance for accident victims as a special act of charity. The financial condition of the *Verein* was not too bad: the deficit in fact had been worse at the end of 1936. However, the questions of new diocesan dissolutions and taxation left the future uncertain.

The suffragan bishop from Trier spoke with urgency about creating a Reich office concerned with youth and urged that concrete economic support for that office be fully mapped out. He sought immediate attention to this matter pointing out that when the *Jugendhaus Düsseldorf, e.V.*, ceased to exist, alternate means had to be available for the new administrative core, the tasks of which were now fulfilled by the *Jugendhaus* and *Bundeshaus*.

The bishop of Mainz prepared a series of resolutions to submit to the episcopate; upon receiving their opinions, he intended to take the results to Rome for final instructions. The resolutions, cast in the form of questions, asked whether the JMV should be retained; whether a dissolution, if there was to be one, should be undertaken only by the entire episcopate; whether a Reich office should be set up for the spiritual care of youth; whether, lacking other means, the diocese should support it by contributions; and whether the bishop of Mainz should create this office subject to the final decision of the Fulda conference.

On November 19, two of the special divisions of the JMV reflected the new spirit in their change of names: the *Sturmschar* became the Community of St. Michael and the *St. Georg Pfadfinderschaft* became the Community of St. Georg. That same day, the JMV in the governmental region of Breslau, which included part but not all of the diocese of Breslau, was dissolved; on November 27, the diocesan JMV of Limburg was dissolved, and also the diocesan group of *Neudeutschland*. The police had already closed *Neudeutschland*'s Castle Raesfeld in September. On February 1, 1938, the great diocesan organizations of the JMV in Cologne and Aachen were dissolved.

The remaining groups in Bavaria were being systematically eliminated. Meanwhile the *Jugendhaus* in Düsseldorf was in chaos because the secret police had made off with its business records, for the alleged purpose of continuing the taxation inquiry.

On June 28, 1938, the *Generalpräsidium* of the JMV met once again in Cologne. Repressive actions against the great diocesan groups had left the JMV with a tenth of its original membership. The Reich office for the spiritual care of youth had been established in Mainz and had made a beginning, although its position was not very firm, since a general recognition of its importance was lacking.

The *Generalpräsidium* was informed of how the JMV was liquidating its property. *Haus Altenberg* had been formally transferred to the archiepiscopal See of Cologne on January 1, 1938; a bookstore with 17,000 volumes had been sold to the See, despite the fact that at the moment is was held by the Gestapo; a boathouse in Düsseldorf had been sold, and also a large Mercedes; the *Jugendbank* had been liquidated without losses. A welfare fund of 10,000 RM had been set up for employees of the JMV and transferred to a trustee. Attempts to transfer *Die Wacht* and *Am Scheideweg* to other presses for safety had proved futile: no press was that intrepid. The circulation of the journals was holding up, however, despite the suppression of the diocesan organizations. Fiscal viability was almost, but not quite nil. Although a bill for taxes had finally been presented, and the figure set at 450,000 RM, appeal of the assessments was expected to produce a reduction to a figure more than covered by the property already seized by the tax office.

The old query was again raised. Should the JMV carry on? This time, the answer was no. There was no will to carry on under the prevaling conditions. In order to salvage the economic basis for its spiritual tasks, the *Generalspräsidium* proposed voluntary dissolution of the Reich office and the remaining diocesan groups of the JMV.

The Vatican had opposed dissolution unless it proved necessary, and unless the episcopate agreed to it unanimously. Apparently, the stipulated conditions were not met, for in the end the decision was left to the police. On September 26, 1938, with typical Nazi legalism, the Gestapo forbade the distribution of *Die Wacht* and *Am*

Scheideweg in dioceses where the JMV had been dissolved. Then on February 6, 1939, a month before the first executive order was issued implementing the Hitler Youth Law, the Gestapo dissolved the JMV and confiscated its goods. The man most responsible for its continued existence, its great protector Piux XI, died four days later.

CONCLUSION

With the German youth movement, a new mode of communal life emerged in the world, a life and spirit which this study has followed to its formal suppression. The Catholic youth leaders adopted this group milieu as an effective means of Christian education. The presence in their organizations of fresh hope and solidarity among the young, and the attendant renewal of all their activities led to direct conflict with the Hitler Youth, itself an offshoot of the autonomous youth movement, although in its first phase it was much more of an SA for adolescents, and in its last phase a ponderous state apparatus for the physical education, disciplining, and indoctrinating of the growing generation. The chronological scope of this study lies between the two phases: when the Hitler Youth was much more than a party youth and yet still less than a state youth; and when its totalistic claims were gradually and fully implemented, it wished to deny to all counterpart groups the activities deriving from the autonomous movement, from the gymnastic and sports associations, and in the end did so, by liquidating the groups themselves. That the Catholic youth organizations held out longest against the Hitler Youth assaults must of course be ascribed first to their formidable aegis the Catholic Church, and to its intangible resources, beside which the puny defense raised by the autonomous youth groups when they rallied behind Admiral Trotha, and the ineffectual defenses of the Evangelical Church, can only be seen as negligible.

The less basic explanations seem all related to this paramount factor. First, as a result of Bismarck's *Kulturkampf,* the Catholics of Germany had formed more of a united bloc than the Protestants, and looked to their priests as the manifest leaders of their interests.[1] Secondly, the attitude of the Church had prevented Catholic clergy from taking an active part in the Nazi party, and when the time came to resist the total extension of the state, the clergy of the Catholic Church were more fully prepared to do so than those of the Evangelical Church, who were deeply divided. Third, the Catholic Church was an international and supranational entity. Its head was not a German national, and he was subject neither to the direct coercion of secular powers nor to the struggle of conscience suffered by the devout Germans torn between allegiance to the state and adherence to the Church.   Since the Pope's concerns and responsibilities were more extensive, profound, and historically distinct than those of the leaders of any political units, and since the seat of ultimate authority in the Church lay outside Germany, the harm which could be incurred through those bishops who wished to throw themselves wholeheartedly into the work of "national reconstruction" was limited.

A final source of strength for the youth organizations was the members themselves.   Their courage in upholding their organizations under stringent pressures probably owed much to religious factors, particularly the incorporation within the Catholic Church of suffering and martyrdom for the faith.   But that it also owed something to the sense of community developed in the course of their evolution, seems implicit in the fact that the groups which collapsed in the first on-slaught in the summer of 1933 were those most recently established and with shallowest roots.[2] Through the personal support of the Pope and the intrepidity of the leaders and members, the organized Catholic youth managed to survive as an enclave of resistance for several years after the Nazi seizure of power.   It was worth the effort, not only because any resolution to resist the spread of totalitarianism is in itself defensible, but because as long as they endured, the youth structure continued to provide an incomparable moral and religious experience for their members.   The morale of the young actually soared under adversity, when outright persecution put character and faith to the test.

The influence of the Catholic youth movement has manifested itself especially in the ranks of the priests of Germany, but it also figured in the development of a surge of renewal within the laity.[3] If, as the Protestant theologian Robert McAfee Brown of Stanford University once said, the spirit of reform today has been most con-spicuous in the Catholic Church, this must be at least partly owing to the youth movement's role within that broad resurgence, particularly in the dissemination of the liturgical movement.

Our own time has witnessed a ferment among the young not without parallel in the history of the German youth movement.   There are theologians and historians who have seen in the extreme youth rebellion of the 1960's a 'religious"—or at the very least an antimundane—spirit manifesting itself. Be that as it may, we are constantly reminded of the sometimes harsh idealism of youth and its search for a meaningful identification in modern mass societies. The Catholic Church was able to capture some of the moral zeal and deep sense of communality of an earlier youth trend and infuse them with religious purposes. It is at least worth wondering whether this or some other institution or source can so organically capture, direct, and endue with more reasonable form the present more frenetic spirit moving youth.

APPENDIX I

List of Microfilm Rolls

Microfilm rolls filmed by the Committee on Research of the American Historical Association, listed in the *Guides to German Records Microfilmed at Alexandria, Va.*, and deposited in the National Archives, Washington, D. C.

Roll	Serial	Microcopy	Guide	Pages in Guide
38	—	T-580	*	—
101	185	T-81	3	57
184	402	T-81	3	124-25
193	193	T-175	33	69-70
409	409	T-175	39	103-04
410	410	T-175	39	106-08
640	855	T-81	35	1-2

* Roll 999 of T-580 serves as a finding guide for that microcopy series.

APPENDIX II

The Hitler Law of December 1, 1936

The future of the German *Volk* depends upon the youth. The whole German youth must therefore be prepared for its future duties. The Reich government therefore has decided upon the following law, which is published herewith:

1. The whole German youth inside of the region of the Reich is incorporated into the Hitler Youth.

161

2. The whole German youth, outside of home and school, is physically, spiritually, and morally to be educated in the Hitler Youth in the spirit of National Socialism to the service of *Volk* and *Volk* community.

3. The task of the education of the whole German youth in the Hitler Youth is given over to the Reich Youth Leader of the NSDAP. He is thereby "Youth Leader of the German Reich." He holds the office of a Highest Reich Authority with its seat in Berlin and is directly responsible to the Führer and Reich Chancellor.

4. The legal orders and general administrative regulations requisite to the execution and completion of this law will be issued by the Führer and Reich Chancellor.

BIBLIOGRAPHY

I. Documents

Albrecht, Dieter, ed. *Der Notenwechsel zwischen dem Heiligen Stuhl und der deutschen Reichsregierung.* Vol. I. *Von der Ratifizierung des Reichskonkordats bis zur Enzyklika "Mit brennender Sorge."* Mainz, 1965.

Baynes, Norman H. *The Speeches of Adolf Hitler April 1922-August 1939.* 2vols. London, 1942.

Bundesarchiv der Deutschen Republik. These materials were filmed for the author and are now deposited at the Library of the University of California, Berkeley. The original documents are deposited at the *Bundesarchiv* of the German Republic, Koblenz. The files consist of some correspondence of the *Reichjugend-führer* and of issues of the *Verordnungsblatt* (later *Nachtrichten-blatt*) *der Reichsjugendführung.*

Corsten, Wilhelm, ed. *Kölner Aktenstücke zur Lage der katholischen Kirche in Deutschland 1933-1945.* Cologne, 1949.

Germany, Auswärtiges Amt. *Documents on German Foreign Policy.* Microcopy T-120, serial 8115, rolls 3310 and 3311.

Germany, Auswärtiges Amt. *Documents on German Foreign Policy 1918-1945.* Series C (1933-1937) and Series D (1937-1945). Washington, 1949-.

Great Britain, Foreign Office. *Documents of British Foreign Policy 1919-1939.* Second Series. London, 1946-.

Hauptarchiv der Nationalsozialistische Deutsche Arbeiter-Partei. These materials have been filmed by the Hoover Institution, Stanford, California. The original documents are deposited at the *Bundesarchiv,* Koblenz.

Hitler, Adolf. *Hitler's Secret Conversations, 1941-1944.* New York, 1953.

Hofer, Walther. *Der Nationalsozialismus Dokumente 1933-1945.* Frankfurt, 1957.

International Military Tribunal. *Trial of the Major War Criminals before the International Military Tribunal.* 42 vols. Nuremberg, 1947-49.

Kindt, Werner. *Grundschriften der Deutschen Jugendbewegung.* Düsseldorf, 1963.

Kupper, Alfons. *Staatliche Akten über die Reichskonkordatsverhandlungen 1933.* Mainz, 1966.

Mosse, George. *Nazi Culture.* New York, 1966.

Müller, Hans. *Katholische Kirche und National Sozialismus, Dokumente 1930-1935.* Munich, 1963.

Neuhäusler, Johann. *Kreuz und Hakenkreuz; der Kampf der Nationalsozialismus gegen die katholische Kirche und der Kirchliche Widerstand.* 2 vols. in 1. Munich, 1946.

The Persecution of the Catholic Church in the Third Reich; facts and documents translated from the German. Published anonymously. London, 1940.

Portmann, Heinrich, ed. *Bishop Graf von Galen Spricht; ein Apostolischer Kampf und sein Widerhall.* Freiburg, 1946.

Rosenberg, Alfred. *Das politische Tagebuch Alfred Rosenbergs aus den Jahren 1934/1935 und 1939/1940.* (Edited by Hans-Günther Seraphim). Göttingen, 1956.

Roth, Heinrich, ed. *Katholische Jugend in der N-S Zeit unter besonder Berücksichtigung des Katholischen Jungmännerverbandes; Daten und Dokumente.* Altenberger Dokumente, Heft 7. Düsseldorf, 1959.

United States, Office of the Chief of Counsel for Prosecution of the Major War Criminals before the International Military Tribunal. *Nazi Conspiracy and Aggresssion.* 10 vols. Washington, 1946-48.

Zipfel, Friedrich. *Kirchenkampf in Deutschland 1933-1945.* Berlin, 1965.

II. Newspapers

The New York Times. New York.

Völkischer Beobachter. Berlin.

Osservatore Romano. Rome.

III. Memoirs

Charles-Roux, Francois. *Huit ans au Vatican, 1932-1940.* Paris, 1947.

Papen, Franz von. *Memoirs.* London, 1952.

Zender, Johannes N. *Neudeutschland. Erinnerungen.* Freiburg, 1949.

IV. Dissertations

Jovy, Ernst Michael. "Deutsche Jugendbewegung und Nationalsozialismus. Versuch einer Klärung ihrer Zusammenhänge und Gegensätze." Unpublished Ph.D. dissertation, Cologne, 1952. Microfilm copy in Hoover Institution.

Lewin, Herbert S. "A Comparative Study of the Principles and Practices of the Hitler Youth and of the Boy Scouts of America." Unpublished Ph.D. dissertation, New School for Social Research, 1947.

Pross, Harry. "Nationale und soziale Prinziples in der Bündische Jugend." Unpublished Ph.D. dissertation, University of Heidelberg, 1949.

Riede, David Charles. "The Official Attitude of the Roman Catholic Hierarchy in Germany Toward National Socialism 1933-45." Unpublished dissertation, State University of Iowa, 1957.

Schmid, Robert Carl. "German Youth Movements: a typological study." Unpublished Ph.D. dissertation, University of Wisconsin, 1941.

V. Articles

Anderson, Eugene N. "German Intellectual History." *Journal of World History*, Vol. II, no. 1 (July, 1954), 214-218.

Aretin, Karl Otmarr Frhr. von. "Prälat Kaas, Franz von Papen und das Reichskonkordat von 1933." *Vierteljahrshefte für Zeitgeschichte*. 14. Jahrgang (July, 1966), 252-279.

Bettelheim, Bruno. "The Problem of Generations." *Daedàlus*, Vol. 91, no. 1 (Winter, 1962), 68-96.

Böckenförde, Ernst-Wolfgang. "German Catholicism in 1933." *Cross Currents*, Vol. XI, no. 3 (Summer, 1961), 283-304.

Buchheim, Hans. "Der deutsche Katholizismus in Jahr 1933." *Hochland*, Vol. 53 (1960-61), 497-515.

Buchheim, Karl. "Warum das Zentrum unterging." *Hochland*, Vol. 53, no. 1 (October 1960), 15-27.

Dorpalen, Andreas. "Wilhelmian Germany—A House Divided Against Itself." *Journal of Central European Affairs*, Vol. XV, no. 3 (October, 1955), 240-247.

Erikson, Erik Homburger. "Hitler's Imagery and German Youth." *Psychiatry*, Vol. V, no. 4 (November, 1942), 475-493.

Harcourt, Robert d'. "National-Socialism and the Catholic Church in Germany," in International Council for Philosophy and Humanistics Studies, *The Third Reich.* New York, 1955, 797-810.

Harrigan, William M. "Nazi Germany and the Holy See, 1933-1936: The Historical Background of Mit Brennender Sorge." *Catholic Historical Review*, Vol. 48 (July, 1961), 164-198.

——————. "Pius XI and Nazi Germany." *Catholic Historical Review*, Vol. 51 (January 1966), 457-486.

——————. "Pius XII's Efforts to Effect a Detente in German-Vatican Relations, 1939-1940." *Catholic Historical Review*, Vol. 49 (July, 1963), 173-191.

Jantzen, Walther. "Die soziologische Herkunft der Führungsschicht der deutschen Jugendbewegung 1900-1933." *Führungsschicht und Eliteproblem.* Jahrbuch III der Ranke-Gesellschaft. Frankfurt, 1957, 127-135

Klönne, Arno. "Die Hitlerjugendgeneration; Bemerkungen zu den politischen Folgen der Staatsjugend Erziehung im Dritten Reich." *Politische Studien*, Heft 106, 10 jahrgang, February, 1959, 93-99.

Kupper, Alfons. "Zur Geschichte des Reichskonkordat." *Stimmen der Zeit*, Vol. 163 (1959/60), 273-302, and 354-371. Vol. 171 (1962/63), 25-50.

Leiber, Robert S.J. "Reichskonkordat und Ende der Zentrumspartei." *Stimmen der Zeit*, Vol. 167 (1960/61), 213-223.

Lewin, Herbert S. "Hitler Youth and the Boy Scouts of America; A Comparison of Aims." *Human Relations*, Vol. I, no. 2 (November, 1947), 206-227.

Lowenthal, Richard. "Communism and Nationalism." *Problems of Communism*, Vol. 10, no. 6 (November-December, 1962), 37-44.

Mason, John Brown. "The Catholic Church and Hitlerism." (Philadelphia, 1933). Reprinted from the *Ecclesiastical Review*, Vol. VIII, no. 4 (April, 1933).

Mau, Hermann. "Die deutsche Jugendbewegung; Rückblick und Ausblick." *Pädagogik*, Heft 7, 2. Jahrgang (July, 1947), 17-27.

Morsey, Rudolf. "Briefe zum Reichskonkordat: Ludwig Kaas—Franz v. Papen." *Stimmen der Zeit*, Vol. 167 (1960/61) 11-30.

——————. "Tagebuch 7. -20. April 1933: Ludwig Kaas." *Stimmen der Zeit*, Vol. 166 (1959/60), 422-430.

Paetel, Karl O. "Die deutsche Jugendbewegung als politisches Phänomen." *Politische Studien*, Heft 86, 8 Jahrgang (June, 1957), 1-14.

Parsons, Talcott. "Democracy and the Social Structure in Pre-Nazi Germany." *Journal of Legal and Political Sociology*, Vol. 1, no. 1-2 (October, 1942), 96-114.

Raabe, Felix. "Bündische Jugend in der Weimarer Republik." *Politische Studien*, Heft 141, 13 Jahrgang (January-February, 1962), 34-41.

Schmidt, Ulrike. "Über das Verhältnis von Jugendbewegung und Hitlerjugend." *Geschichte in Wissenschaft und Unterricht*, Jan. 1965, 19-37.

Zahn, Gordon. "The German Catholic Press and Hitler's Wars." *Cross Currents*, Vol. X, no. 4 (Fall, 1960), 337-351.

VI. Books

Adolf, Walter. *Hirtenamt und Hitler-Diktatur*. Berlin, 1965.

Becker, Howard. *German Youth: Bond or Free*. New York, 1946.

Bettelheim, Bruno. *The Informed Heart; Autonomy in a Mass Age*. Glencoe, Illinois, 1961.

Binder, Gerhart. *Irrtum und Widerstand; die deutschen Katholiken in der Auseinandersetzung mit dem Nationalsozialismus*. Munich, 1968.

Bracher, Karl Dietrich. *Nationsozialistische Machtergreifung und Reichskonkordat*. Wiesbaden, 1956.

Buchheim, Hans. *Glaubenskrise im Dritten Reich.* Stuttgart, 1953.

Conrad, Walter. *Der Kampf um die Kanzeln; Erinnerungen und Dokumente aus der Hitlerzeit.* Berlin, 1957.

Conway, John S. *Nazi Persecution of the Churches.* London, 1968.

Davidson, Eugene. *The Trial of the Germans: an Account of the Twenty-two Defendants before the International Military Tribunal at Nuremberg.* New York, 1966.

Deuerlin, Ernst. *Der deutsche Katholizismus 1933.* Osnabrück, 1963.

—————————. *Das Reichskonkordat. Beitrage zur Vorgeschichte, Abschluss und Vollzug der Konkordates zwischen dem Heiligen Stuhl und dem Deutschen Reich vom 20. Juli 1933.* Düsseldorf, 1956.

Donohoe, James *Hitler's Conservative Opponents in Bavaria, 1930-1945; A Study of Catholic, Monarchist and Separatist Anti-Nazi Activities.* Leiden, 1961.

Duncan-Jones, A.S. *The Struggle for Religious Freedom in Germany.* London, 1938.

Erikson, Erik H. *Childhood and Society.* New York, 1950.

—————————. *Identity: Youth and Crisis.* New York, 1968.

Fick, Luise. *Die Deutsche Jugendbewegung.* Jena, 1939.

Gallin, Mary Alice. *German Resistance to Hitler: Ethical and Religious Factors.* Washington, D. C., 1962.

Groppe, Herbert. *Das Reichskonkordat vom 20 July 1933; eine Studie zur staats-und völker-rechtlichen Bedeutung dieses Vertrages für die Bundesrepublik Deutschland.* Cologne, 1956.

Hale, Oron J. *The Captive Press in the Third Reich.* Princeton, New Jersey, 1964.

Harcourt, Robert d'. *The German Catholics.* London, 1939.

Hederer, Josef. *Die Jugendgemeinschaften und ihre Führer, eine historische Darsellung.* Neubiberg and Munich, 1959.

Helmreich, Ernst Christian. *Religious Education in German Schools; an Historical Approach.* Cambridge, Mass., 1959.

Hitler, Adolf. *Mein Kampf.* New York, 1939.

Horkenbach, Cuno. *Das Deutsche Reich von 1918 bis heute, 1933*. 3 vols. Berlin, 1930-35.

International Council for Philosophy and Humanistic Studies. *The Third Reich*. New York, 1955.

Kellerman, Henry J. *The Present Status of German Youth*. United States Department of State Publication 2583, European Series 11, Washington, D. C. 1946.

Klemperer, Klemens von. *Germany's New Conservatism: Its History and Dilemma in the Twentieth Century*. Princeton, 1957.

Klönne, Arno. *Gegen den Strom; der Widerstand der Jugend gegen Hitler*. Hanover and Frankfurt, 1960.

——————. *Hitlerjugend; die Jugend und ihre Organisation im Dritten Reich*. Hanover and Frankfurt, 1960.

Klose, Werner. *Generation im Gleichschritt; ein Dokumentarbericht*. Oldenburg, 1964.

Korn, Elisabeth; Suppert, Otto; and Vogt, Karl, eds. *Die Jugendbewegung; Wert und Wirkung*. Düsseldorf, 1963.

Laqueur, Walter Z. *Young Germany; A History of the German Youth Movement*. London, 1962.

Lersner, Dieter Freiherr von. *Die evangelischen Jugendverbände Württembergs und die Hitler-Jugend 1933-1934*. Göttingen, 1958.

Lewy, Guenther. *The Catholic Church and Nazi Germany*. New York, 1964.

Lipset, Seymour Martin. *Political Man: The Social Bases of Politics*. Garden City, New York, 1963.

Maccarrone, Michele. *Il Nazionalsocialismo e la Santa Sede*. Rome, 1947.

Macfarland, C. S. *The New Church and the New Germany: a Study of Church and State*. New York, 1934.

Mason, John Brown. *Hitler's First Foes; a study in Religion and Politics*. Minneapolis, 1936.

Masur, Gerhard. *Prophets of Yesterday: Studies in European Culture, 1890-1914.* New York, 1966.

Matthias, Erich and Morsey, Rudolf, eds. *Das Ende der Parteien 1933.* Düsseldorf, 1960.

Mickelm, Nathaniel. *National Socialism and the Roman Catholic Church, 1933-1938.* London, 1939.

Nisbet, Robert A. *Community and Power.* New York, 1962.

————. *The Sociological Tradition.* New York, 1966.

Paetel, Karl Otto. *Das Bild vom Menschen in der Deutschen Jugendführung.* Bad Godesberg, 1954.

Portmann, Henrich. *Cardinal von Galen.* London, 1957.

Priepke, Manfred. *Die Evangelische Jugend im Dritten Reich, 1933-1936.* Hanover and Frankfurt, 1960.

Raabe, Felix. *Die bündische Jugend; ein Betrag zur Geschichte der Weimarer Republik.* Stuttgart, 1961.

Rauschning, Hermann. *The Voice of Destruction.* New York, 1940.

Roessler, Wilhelm. *Jugend im Erziehungsfeld.* Düsseldorf, 1957.

Schirach, Baldur von. *Die Hitler-Jugend; Idee und Gestalt.* Berlin, 1934.

Schneider-Schelde, Rudolf, ed. *Die Frage der Jugend; Aufsätze, Berichte, Briefe und Reden.* Munich, 1946.

Steward, John S. *Sieg des Glaubens; Authentische Gestapoberichte über den kirchlichen Widerstand in Deutschland.* Zürich, 1946.

Vagts, Alfred. *Hitler's Second Army.* Washington, D. C., 1943.

Volk, Ludwig. *Der Bayerische Episkopat und der National Sozialismus 1930-1934.* Mainz, 1966.

Zahn, Gordon. *German Catholics and Hitler's Wars.* New York, 1962.

NOTES

List of Abbreviations

Bayerischer Episkopat	Ludwig Volk. *Der Bayerische Episkopat und der National Sozialismus 1930-1934.* Mainz, 1966.
BDR	*Bundesarchiv der Deutschen Republic.* This abbreviation indicates the material cited is deposited at the *Bundesarchiv* of the German Republic, Koblenz, and was filmed for the author. The films are now deposited at the Library of the University of California, Berkeley. These rolls were filmed without frame numbers.
DGFP	Germany, Auswärtiges Amt. *Documents on German Foreign Policy 1918-1945* (Washington, 1949-). Volumes from Series C (1933-1937) and Series D (1937-1945) are cited in this work. The letter of the Series and the volume number are cited in abbreviated form: C1 refers to Series C, volume 1.
DGFP Film	Selected documents were filmed for the use of the editors-in-chief of *Documents on German Foreign Policy.* These films, which are now available, contain documents not published in the edited series. Used here are T-120, serial 8115, rolls 3310 and 3311. A brief description of the contents of these rolls is contained in Stanford University, Hoover Institution on War, Revolution and Peace, *A Catalog of Files and Microfilms of the German Foreign Ministry Archives, 1920-1945,* Vol. I (Stanford, Calif., 1962), p. 141. Much of this material is now available in *Notenwechsel.*
IMT	International Military Tribunal, *Trial of the Major War Criminals before the International Military Tribunal,* 42 vols., (Nuremberg, 1947-49).

171

Kath. Jung.   Heinrich Roth, ed., *Katholische Jugend in der N-S Zeit unter besonder Berücksichtigung des Katholischen Jungmännerverbandes; Daten und Dokumente* (Düsseldorf, 1959). This volume contains two sections, a section listing events chronologically (the *Regesten*) and a document section. The *Regesten* lists some events for which no documents were published. On the other hand, some documents were printed which have no relation to the *Regesten.* Usually, however, the two sections must be used together. Source references for the documents are usually contained in the *Regesten.* The documents are often divided into sections and the parts arranged under various chapter headings. Material in the *Regesten* is abbreviated in this text as *Reg., * followed by the *Regesten number.* Documents are cited by the pages on which they appear.

Kirche und NS   Hans Müller, *Katholische Kirche und National Sozialismus, Dokumente 1930-1935* (Munich, 1963).

Kirchenkampf   Friedrich Zipfel. *Kirchenkampf in Deutschland 1933-1945.* (Berlin, 1965).

Köln. Akt.   Wilhelm Corsten, ed., *Kölner Aktenstücke zur Lage der katholischen Kirche in Deutschland 1933-1945* (Cologne, 1949).

Kreuz.   Johann Neuhäusler, *Kreuz und Hakenkreuz; der Kampf des Nationalsozialismus gegen die katholische Kirche und der kirchliche Widerstand*, 2 vols. in 1, (Munich, 1946).

NA   American Historical Association, Committee for the Study of War Documents. The committee has prepared a series of *Guides to German records microfilmed at Alexandria, Va.* (Washington, D. C., 1958-). The reels are available from the National Archives, Washington, D. C. Footnotes cite the roll number and the frames used, except in the case of T-copy 580, roll 38, which was filmed without frame numbers and for which a guide has not yet been published. A table in the Appendix indicates serial numer, the number of the Guide in which the contents of the rolls are described, and the pages in the Guide bearing the description of the roll's contents.

NCA	United States, Office of the Chief of Counsel for Prosecution of the Major War Criminals before the International Military Tribunal, *Nazi Conspiracy and Aggression,* 10 vols., (Washington, 1946-48).
Notenwechsel	Dieter Albrecht, ed. *Der Notenwechsel zwischen dem Heiligen Stuhl und der deutschen Reichsregierung.* Vol. I. *Von der Ratifizierung des Reichskonkordats bis zur Enzyklika "Mit brennender Sorge."* Mainz, 1965.
NS Hauptarchiv	*Hauptarchiv der Nationsozialistische Deutsche Arbeiter-Partei.* This abbreviation refers to materials collected by the *Hauptarchiv* of the Nazi Party which were filmed by Hoover Institution, Stanford, California. The original documents are deposited at the *Bundesarchiv,* Koblenz. There are no frame numbers on these rolls.
Persec.	*The Persecution of the Catholic Church in the Third Reich; facts and documents translated from the German* (London, 1940). Published anonymously.
RK	Ernst Deuerlein. *Das Reichskonkordat. Beitrage zur Vorgeschichte, Abschluss und Vollzug der Konkordates zwischen dem Heiligen Stuhl und dem Deutschen Reich vom 20. Juli 1933* (Düsseldorf, 1956).
Zentrumspartei	Matthias, Erich and Morsey, eds. *Das Ende der Parteien 1933,* Düsseldorf, 1960.

NOTES

Chapter One

1. Erik H. Erikson, "Hitler's Imagery and German Youth," *Psychiatry*, Vol. V, no. 4 (November, 1942), pp. 478-79. The contents of the article have been reproduced in Chapter 9 of *Childhood and Society*.
2. Bruno Bettelheim, "The Problem of Generations," *Daedalus*, Vol. 91, no. 1 (winter, 1962), pp. 93-94.
3. This idea has been developed by Robert C. Schmid, "German Youth Movements: a typological Study," (Unpublished Ph.D. thesis, University of Wisconsin, 1941), pp. 268-73.
4. This was double the percentage of losses (one eighth) suffered by the army as a whole. Luise Fick, *Die deutsche Jugendbewegung* (Jena, 1939), p. 243, n. 1.
5. Hermann Mau, "Die deutsche Jugendbewegung; Ruckblick und Ausblick," *Pädagogik*, 2. Jahrgang, Heft 7 (July, 1947), p. 23. The article is fundamental to an understanding of the spirit of the youth movement.

Chapter Two

1. Mau, pp. 17-27.
2. Knud Ahlborn, "Das Meissnerfest der Freideutschen Jugend," in Werner Kindt, *ed., Grundschriften der Deutschen Jugendbewegung* (Düsseldorf-Köln, 1963), p. 109. Howard Becker, *German Youth: Bond or Free* (New York, 1946) translates the formula as follows: "Free German Youth, on their initiative, under their own responsibility, and with deep sincerity, are determined independently to shape their own lives. For the sake of this inner freedom they will under any and all circumstances take united action. . . ." Klemens von Klemperer in his *Germany's New Conservation* (Princeton, 1957), p. 46, n. 9, cites the account of A. Messer, *Die freideutsche Jugendbewegung* (Gotha, 1920), pp. 27ff. that the last sentence and the words "on their own initiative" were omitted after a March 1914 meeting at Marburg where the moderates prevailed. Nevertheless, it is a

175

bold statement in either form and had a shock effect upon the older generation. Johannes Zender, *Neudeutschland* (Freiburg, 1949), p. 14, quotes the Meissner declaration, apparently incorrectly, but revealingly in terms of his own reaction: "Youth will shape their own lives, under their own responsibility, independent of School, Home, and Church."

3. *NS Hauptarchiv*, Roll 18.

4. Lenk to the Schriftleiter des Völkischen Beobachter, Munich, April 22, 1925 (Enclosure, "Nationalsozialistische Jugendbewegung"), *NA*, roll 38.

5. Lenk to Udo Pfriemer, Munich, June 13, 1933, *NS Hauptarchiv,* roll 18.

6. Rossbach to the Partei-Leitung, Salzburg, April 28, 1925, *NA,* roll 38.

7. Lenk to Udo Pfriemer, Munich, June 13, 1933, *NS Hauptarchiv,* roll 18.

8. Rossbach to the Partei-Leitung, Salzburg, April 28, 1925, *NA,* roll 38.

9. Der Reichsjugendführer to the Gebietsführer der Hitlerjugend, Bundesführer Jungvolk, and Bundesführer N.S.D.St.B., Munich, October 7, 1932, *NA*, roll 38.

10. "Jahresberichte der Hitlerjugend für die Zeit vom 1. Januar 1931 zum 31 Dezember 1931," Munich, February 1, 1932, *NA,* roll 38.

11. Felix Raabe, *Die Bündische Jugend* (Stuttgart, 1961), p. 170.

12. Baldur von Schirach, *Die Hitler-Jugend: Idee und Gestalt* (Leipzig, 1934), p. 13.

13. *Ibid.*, pp. 51 and 49.

14. *Ibid.*, p. 25.

15. The Sozialreferent HJ to the Reichsorganisationsleiter of the NSDAP (Munich), November 2, 1932, *BDR*, roll no. 1.

16. *Verordnungsblatt der Reichsjugendführung* (Hitler-Jugend), Vol. III, no. 15 (April 25, 1935), p. 2, *BDR*, roll no. 1.

17. *Ibid.*, no. 17 (May 9, 1935), p. 2.

18. *Ibid.*, no. 18 (May 16, 1935), pp. 4-6.

19. *Ibid.*, no. 38 (October 24, 1935), p. 5.

20. Schirach, *Die Hitler-Jugend*, p. 42.

21. Walter Dirks, "Anfänge und Folgen katholischer Jugendbewegung," in Elisabeth Korn, *et al.*, eds., *Die Jugendbewegung; Welt and Wirkung* (Düsseldorf, 1963), pp. 243-245.

22. Romano Guardini, "Quickborn—Tatsachen und Grundstätze," in Kindt, *ed.*, *Grundschriften der Deutschen Jugendbewegung*, pp. 335-50.

23. Johannes Zender, *Neudeutschland* (Freiburg im Breisgau, 1949), p. 16.

24. *Ibid.*, pp. 25-27. As early as the summer of 1933 Cardinal Schulte advised Father Zender that *Neudeutschland* was finished. *Ibid.*, p. 224.

25. *Ibid.*, p. 206.

26. *Kath. Jung.*, pp. 185-86.

27. Dirks, *op. cit.*, pp. 248-49; Zender, *Neudeutschland*, pp. 50-51 and 189-96.

28. Der Reichsführer SS, Der Chef des Sicherheitshauptamtes, *Sonderbericht: Das katholische Vereinwesen: Die Organization der katholischen Jugendvereine* (September, 1935), *NA*, serial 410, roll 410, frame 2934786. In most years, between 1,000,000 and 1,200,000 boys and girls graduated from schools. In 1930, there were only 793,000 graduates; in 1931, 700,000; in 1932, 650,000; and in 1933, 695,000. In 1934 the figure would rise to about 1,300,000. *Osservatore Romano*, April 27, 1934, 1:1.

29. The five German dioceses with the highest JMV membership were 1) Münster with 67,409 members, representing 38.7% of the eligible youth of the diocese; 2) Cologne with 49,830, 20.6% of the young Catholics; 3) Paderborn with 47,120, or 30% and 4) Trier with 34,660, representing 23.5 % and 5) Aachen with 29,900 and 25.9%. Of those dioceses with lesser membership, the diocese of Osnabrück with 16,620 showed itself extremely successful in having organized 37.6% of the youth. Some of the poorest showings were in southern Germany, parts of which the JMV had scarcely penetrated. For example the diocese of Munich-Freising had 4200 members, which represented

a mere 3.2% of the eligible youth. Apparently efforts were being made at the *Jungschar* level though, because of the total membership, 72.14% were in the youngest age group. *Sonderbericht,* frame 2934789. These diocesan figures include the total membership of the JMV for the diocese, including members over 17 years of age.

30. *Sonderbericht,* frame 2934795. By December 1935 the circulation of *Michael* had climbed to 300,000. *Kath. Jung.,* p. 227, fn. 79.

31. *NA,* serial 193, frames 2932595-630 and 2732786-818.

32. *Ibid.,* frame 2732102.

Chapter Three

1. Hans Buchheim, *Glaubenskrise im Dritten Reich* (Stuttgart, 1953), pp. 9-10 and 36-39.

2. Adolf Hitler, *Mein Kampf* (New York, 1941), pp. 267-69.

3. *Kirche und NS,* p. 119.

4. The letter is quoted in Ernst Christian Helmreich, *Religious Education in German Schools* (Cambridge, Mass., 1959), p. 186.

5. The Sicherheitsdienst Lagebericht Mai/Juni 1934 summed it up. " 'Without Catholic youth, no Catholic future!' it says in a Catholic publication. National Socialism must reply: Without National Socialist youth, no German future! The German future can not be given up in favor of Catholic goals. Thus the decisive battle between National Socialism and Catholicism is played out as a fight over the youth." *Kirchenkampf,* Doc. no. 10, p. 297.

6. *NA,* roll 193, frames 2732634-35 and 2732691.

7. *DGFP,* C3, no. 15, pp. 39-42; no. 213, pp. 417-419, and p. 489, fn. 8. Limitations on Hitler's policy toward the Catholic Church were also imposed by his need not to allenate his potential allies Mussolini's Italy and Franco's Spain. For numerous examples of this see the article by William M. Harrigan, "Pius XII's Efforts to Effect a Detente in German-Vatican Relations, 1939-1940," *Catholic Historical Review,* Vol. 49, no. 2 (July, 1963), p. 181n.

8. *NA,* roll 193, frames 2732373-79, -84, 2732836, 2732915, -18, and -19, 2732362, and roll 410, frame 2933807; roll 193, frame 2732635.

9. Mary Alice Gallin, *German Resistance to Hitler: Ethical and Religious Factors* (Washington, D. C., 1962), p. 217.
10. Guenther Lewy, *The Catholic Church and Nazi Germany* (New York, 1964), p. 319.
11. *NA*, roll 193, frames 2732501-02.
12. *Kath. Jung.*, *Reg.* 63, p. 113; *NA*, roll 193, frame 2732515.
13. Bruno Bettelheim, *The Informed Heart; Autonomy in a Mass Age* (Glencoe, Ill., 1961), pp. 228-229.   1
14. *Kath. Jung.*, p. 103.
15. Gordon Zahn, "The German Catholic Press and Hitler's Wars," *Cross Currents*, Vol. X, no. 4 (Fall, 1960), p. 343.
16. Report of the Bishop of Trier on His Negotiations Concerning the Saar Territory, Rome, November 20, 1933, *DGFP*, C2, no. 96, p. 171.   This same Bishop Börnewasser of Trier on August 28, 1938 was to praise from the pulpit Bishop Sproll for refusing to vote in a plebiscite, an action which caused Bishop Sproll to be barred from his diocese by the government. See *Kirchenkampf*, p. 464.
17. *DGFP*, C4, no. 488, pp. 980-982.
18. Helmreich, *Religious Education*, pp. 153-154.   When the Nazis came to power, the vast majority of schools were "confessional" schools.   Catholic private schools of the type common in America were not common in Germany, and there was little need for them. In a Catholic area, the teachers of the school were customarily Catholic and a local priest might conduct the weekly classes in religion or a Church official might at least occasionally visit the classes.   In a Protestant area, the teachers would normally be Protestant.   This situation made it relatively easy for the Nazis to drive the churches out of the field of education by a strict policy of separating church and state.

Chapter Four

1. Buchheim, *Glaubenskrise*, pp. 64-66.
2. *Kirche und NS*, pp. 13-15.   Article 24 states: "We demand the freedom of all religious confessions in the state insofar as they do not endanger its existence or violate the moral feeling of the Germanic race.   The party as such represents the standpoint of

a positive Christianity, without binding itself to a particular religion. It fights the Jewish-materialistic spirit *within* and *without* ourselves and is convinced that a lasting recovery of our *Volk* can succeed only proceeding from within outward on the basis: *common good before private good.*"

3. Seymour Martin Lipset, *Political Man: the Social Bases of Politics* (Garden City, New York, 1963), pp. 138-139.

4. *Zentrumspartei,* pp. 358-364 and 429-431.

5. Norman H. Baynes, *The Speeches of Adolf Hitler April 1922-August 1939,* (London, 1942), Vol. I, p. 370. The sentence "The National Government will allow and secure to the Christian Confessions the influence which is their due both in the school and in education" was soon dropped from Nazi publications of the speech. See Buchheim, *Glaubenskrise,* pp. 82 and 213, fn. 60.

6. *Zentrumspartei,* p. 364. Msgr. Kaas was very optimistic and enthusiastic. Ludwig Kaas, "Tagebuch 7.-20. April 1933; Aus dem Nachlass von Prälat Ludwig Kaas," edited by Rudolf Morsey *Stimmen der Zeit,* 166, no. 12 (September, 1960), p. 426.

7. Ernst Deuerlein analyzes the reasons for this announcement in *Der deutsche Katholizismus 1933* (Osnabrück,1963), pp. 145-153.

8. *Zentrumspartei,* pp. 371n and 382n.

9. Papen in his testimony before the International Military Tribunal said he suggested the concordat to Hitler, *IMT*, Vol. XVI, p. 281. Rudolf Morsey believes the initial suggestion came from the cardinal secretary of state. Kaas, "Tagebuch," p. 425. Karl Otmar Frhr. von Aretin, "Prälat Kaas, Franz von Papen und das Reichskonkordat von 1933," *Vierteljahrshefte für Zeitgeschichte,* 14 Jahr, 3 Heft (July, 1966), p. 263, denies that the question can be answered at present.

10. *Bayerischer Episkopat,* pp. 111-112; *Der deutsche Katholizismus,* pp. 158-159.

11. Consisting of the *Generalpräses* (Wolker) and *Generalskretär* (Clemens) with the *Diozesanpräsides* of the German dioceses.

12. Consisting of the *Generalpräses, Generalsekretär, Reichsobmann,* one diocesan *Präses,* and four *Jungmännern.*

13. A building constructed by the JMV on land owned by the diocese of Osnabrück used for youth leadership conferences and training courses.

14. *Köln. Akt.*, pp. 9-11.

15. *Bayerischer Episkopat*, pp. 98-99. The order was issued again in September and made even more restrictive. *Notenwechsel,* pp. 3-9.

16. Robert d'Harcourt, *The German Catholics* (London, 1939), pp. 89-90.

17. John Brown Mason, *Hitler's First Foes; a Study in Religion and Politics* (Minneapolis, 1936), pp. 55-56.

18. Karl Dietrich Bracher, *Nationalsozialistische Machtergreifung und Reichskonkordat* (Weisbaden, 1956), p. 60.

19. *Bayerischer Episkopat*, pp. 115-116.

20. Walter Conrad, *Der Kampf um die Kanzeln; Erinnerungen und Dokumente aus der Hitlerzeit* (Berlin, 1957), pp. 36-37.

21. Deuerlein, *Der deutsche Katholizismus*, pp. 121-122.

22. Conrad, *Kampf um die Kanzeln*, pp. 42-43.

23. *Persec.*, p. 85.

24. Michele Maccarrone, *Il Nazionalsocialismo e la Santa Sede* (Rome, 1947), p. 15.

25. *Ibid.*, p. 16.

26. *DGFP*, C1, no. 371, p. 676.

27. Conrad, *Kampf um die Kanzeln*, p. 39.

28. *Persec.*, pp. 85 and 188.

29. Maccarrone, *Il Nazionalsocialismo*, p. 17.

30. *Kirche und NS*, pp. 185-186.

31. *DGFP*, C1, no. 418, p. 783.

Chapter Five

1. *Kath. Jung.*, pp. 62-63.

2. *Kirche und NS*, pp. 180-181.

3. *NCA*, Vol. V, p. 198, 2455PS.

4. *Kath. Jung.*, *Reg.* 18, p. 96, and *Reg.* 29, p. 156.

5. *NA*, roll 101, frames 117669-70.

6. Cardinal Bertram referred to it in a protest to the Foreign Ministry on September 7, 1933. *RK*, p. 307.

7. *Kath. Jung., Reg.* 18, pp. 95-98 and p. 187.

8. *Ibid., Regs.* 25, 26 and 27, pp. 71-72.

9. Conrad, *Kampf um die Kanzeln*, pp. 72-74.

10. *DGFP*, C2, no. 98, p. 173

11. *Kath. Jung.*, p. 74.

12. Nathaniel Mickelm, *National Socialism and the Roman Catholic Church, 1933-1938* (London, 1939), pp. 96-97.

13. Conrad, *Kampf um die Kanzeln*, pp. 77-79.

14. *RK*, p. 138.

15. d'Harcourt, *The German Catholics*, p. 138; *Bayerischer Episkopat*, pp. 152-153.

16. A. S. Duncan Jones, *The Struggle for Religious Freedom in Germany* (London, 1938), p. 165.

17. *DGFP*, C2, no. 64, pp. 113-114.

18. *Bayerischer Episkopat*, p. 163.

19. *DGFP*, C2, p. 114n.

20. Conrad, *Kampf um die Kanzeln*, pp. 105-106.

21. *Kath. Jung., Reg.* 40, pp. 118-119, and p. 221, fns. 58 and 59.

22. *Persec.*, pp. 108-109.

23. *DGFP, Film*, roll 3311, frame E580623.

24. *DGFP*, C2, no. 149, p. 277.

25. *Ibid.*, C2, no. 152, pp. 284-285. Three White Books were eventually prepared covering relations from September 5, 1933 to June 6, 1936 and made available to the bishops, but never published. Their contents have been incorporated in *Notenwechsel.*

Chapter Six

1. *NA*, roll 193, frame 2732676.

2. *Ibid.*, frames 2732930-33.

3. *Ibid.*, frame 2732311.

4. *Ibid.*, frames 2732353-55.

5. In the early years of the regime Archbishop Gröber's enthusiasm for the tasks of the "national renewal" won for him the nickname

"Brown Conrad". He was even made an honorary member of the SS. He could recognize a threat to religion in the long run, however, and he was later deprived of that dubious honor. Deuerlein, *Der deutsche Katholizismus*, pp. 164-165. The Sicherheitsdeinst did not regard Archbishop Gröber with any affection. See *Kirchenkampf*, pp. 277, 293. By 1938 the SD grouped him with Cardinal Faulhaber and Bishop Galen as "malicious enemies of National Socialism," p. 463. He revealed early that despite his naive optimism toward Nazism, he was no racist: "Our Catholic Church is general, therefore not a faith limited by boundaries of a nation, by the walls of one race: it is the church of all peoples and of all times." *Osservatore Romano*, April 8, 1934, 1:4.

6. *Persec.*, p. 14. Time revealed that Bishop Ehrenfried was not sympathetic to the supposed goals of the regime in the manner of Archbishop Gröber, who was summoned to Rome by Msgr. Kaas in May 1934 to serve as a counterpoise to Bishop Ehrenfried and Cardinal Faulhaber who were visiting there. *DGFP*, C2, no. 463, p. 842.

7. *NA*, roll 193, frames 2732847, -85, and -911.

8. Gedanken über Gegenmassnahmen gegen die persönlich oppositionären Geistliches, June 5, 1934, *Ibid.*, frames 2732634-42.

Chapter Seven

1. *NA*, roll 193, frame 2732744.

2. *Kirchenkampf*, p. 62.

3. *Osservatore Romano*, April 26, 1934, 1:2-3.

4. *Köln. Akt.*, p. 19.

5. *DGFP Film*, roll 3310, frame E580282.

6. *Kath. Jung.*, p. 76; *RK*, p. 148.

7. Conrad, *Kampf um die Kanzeln*, pp. 106-108.

8. *RK*, pp. 148-149.

9. *DGFP*, C2, no. 272, p. 519. According to a notation by Heinrich Roth, Papen, Buttmann and Schirach met with Hitler on February 26 to discuss Article 31. *Kath. Jung.*, p. 76.

10. *Kath. Jung.*, pp. 75-76.

11. *Ibid.*, pp. 79-83.
12. *Ibid.*, p. 75.
13. *DGFP Film*, roll 3311, frame E580519.
14. *Ibid.*; *Kath. Jung.*, *Reg.* 39, p. 146.
15. *Kath. Jung.*, *Reg.* 51, pp. 146-147.
16. *NA*, roll 193, frame 2732618. This gave rise to a general "Loyalty epidemic," as the SD termed it, frame 2732687.
17. *Kath. Jung.*, *Regs.* 43, 44 and 45, p. 103.
18. *Ibid.*, *Reg.* 50, pp. 157-58.
19. *NA*, roll 193, frames 2732767-70.

Chapter Eight

1. *DGFP Film*, roll 3311, frames E580618-19.
2. *Ibid.*, frames E580640-50.
3. Maccarrone, *Il Nazionalsocialismo*, pp. 52-57.
4. *Ibid.*, p. 57.
5. *Ibid.*, p. 69.
6. *Ibid.*, p. 70.
7. *Notenwechsel*, p. 145.
8. Schirach, *Die Hitler-Jugend*, p. 40.
9. *DGFP*, C1, no. 278, p. 507.
10. *DGFP*, C2, no. 85, p. 151. Bishop Bares was to show his moral courage at a later date by holding memorial services for Catholic Action's Erich Klausner, whom the Nazis executed and reported as a suicide, *Kirchenkampf*, pp. 65-66. Bishop Bares died on March 1, 1935 and was replaced by Graf von Preysing as bishop of Berlin.
11. *Kirche und NS*, nos. 148 and 149, pp. 290-291. On June 25, 1934 Bishop Berning also requested that a letter to Hitler prepared by Cardinal Faulhaber not be sent, in order not to disturb the negotiations, *Bayerischer Episkopat*, p. 198.
12. Alfred Rosenberg, *Das politische Tagebuch Alfred Rosenbergs aus den Jahren 1934/35 und 1939/40* (Göttingen, 1956), p. 32.
13. *Kirchenkampf*, p. 63.
14. *NA*, roll 193, Frames 2732779-80.

15. *Ibid.*, frame 2732781; *Osservatore Romano*, May 14-15, 1934, 4:4 carries the text.
16. *NA*, roll 193, frame 2732783.
17. *Ibid.*, frames 2732770-72.
18. *Ibid.*, frame 2732786.
19. *Ibid.*, frame 2732624.
20. *Ibid.*, frames 2732775-77.
21. *Ibid.*, frames 2732774-75.
22. *Ibid.*, frame 2732813.
23. *Ibid.*, frame 2732778; *Kath. Jung.*, p. 159.
2⁴. *NA*, roll 193, frame 2732780-83.
25. *Kath. Jung.*, *Reg.* 60.
26. *NA*, roll 193, frames 2732813-14.
27. *Ibid.*, frames 2732788-89. For an SD view of Catholic Action see *Kirchenkampf*, pp. 282-287.
28. *NA*, roll 193, frames 2732624-26.
29. *Ibid.*, frame 2732814.
30. *Ibid.*, frames 2732789-92.
31. *Ibid.*, frame 2732595.
32. *Ibid.*, frame 2732609.
33. *Ibid.*, frames 2732610-19; *Osservatore Romano*; May 31, 1934, 1:1, carries an account of the telegram to the pope.
34. *Ibid.*, frames 2732606-07.
35. *Ibid.*, frames 2732609, -765, -786, and -791.
36. *Ibid.*, frames 2732673 and -786.
37. *Ibid.*, frames 2732671-72 and -674-76.
38. Goering maintained at Nuremberg that he ordered Klausner evecuted for his work in Catholic Action. See *Kirchenkampf*, p. 64.
39. *NA*, roll 193, frames 2732530-43, and *Kath. Jung.*, *Regs.* 67, 70 and 77, pp. 122-23. For an account of services for Erich Klausner see *Kirchenkampf*, pp. 65-66.
40. *NA*, roll 193, frame 2732673.
41. *Ibid.*, frame 2732701.
42. *Ibid.*, frames 2732693-96.

43. *Ibid.*, frame 2732690.

44. *Ibid.*, frames 2732694-700.

45. *Kirchenkampf*, Doc. no. 53, p. 468

46. *NA*, roll 193, frames 2732701-04.

47. The Gestapo in Berlin issued an order on Dec. 7, 1934, limiting pilgrimages to traditional ones, *ibid.*, roll 409, frame 2932671. Dr. Muhs, of the Reich ministry of interior refers to the order in a letter of August 17, 1937 to the German bishops, *ibid.*, roll 184, frame 0333823.

48. *Kirchenkampf*, Doc. no.53, p. 470.

Chapter Nine

1. *Kath. Jung.*, p. 77.   Results of the negotiations had been published, *RK*, p. 161.

2. *DGFP*, C3, no. 50, pp. 109-111.   A brief sketch of the negotiations has been left by Buttmann's Tagebuch, quoted in *RK*, pp. 160-161.

3. Entwurf einer Vereinbarung betr. Ausführung von Art. 31, *DGFP Film*, roll 3311, frame E580764.

4. *DGFP*, C3, no. 50, p. 110.

5. *DGFP Film*, roll 3311, frame E580760.

6. *Ibid.*, roll 3311, frame E580846.

7. *DGFP*, C3, no. 195, pp. 388-389.   The points concerning the youth and workers' associations were written according to instructions from the Pope, *DGFP Film*, roll 3311, frame E580846.

8. Abgeänderter Entwurf einer Vereinbarung betr. Ausführung von Art. 31, *DGFP Film*, roll 3311, frames E580820-25 and Begründung der Abänderungsvorschläge zu dem Entwurf einer Vereinbarung über Artikel 31, frame E580829.

9. The Deputy Director of Department II to the Embassy to the Holy See, September 21, 1934, *DGFP*, C3, no. 216, p. 423.

10. Entry for November 17, 1934 in Buttmann's Tagebuch cited by *RK*, p. 163.

11. Buttmann made one last trip to Rome in June, 1935, with no result.

Chapter Ten

1. *Verordnungsblatt der Reichsjugendführung* (Hitler-Jugend) Vol. III, no. 2, (Jan. 18, 1935), p. 2, *BDR*, roll 1.
2. Helmreich, *Religious Education*, pp. 173-174.
3. Walther Hofer, *Der Nationalsozialismus Dokumente 1933-1945* (Frankfurt, 1957), p. 128.
4. d'Harcourt, *The German Catholics*, p. 168.
5. *Verordnungsblatt*, Vol. II, no. 15 (Sept. 22, 1934), pp. 5-7, *BRD*, roll 1.
6. *Kath. Jung.*, p. 168.
7. *Ibid., Reg.* 94, p. 105
8. *Ibid., Reg.* 95, pp. 104-105.
9. *Persec.*, p. 87.
10. *Kath. Jung.*, p. 168.
11. *NA*, roll 193, frame 2732609.
12. Werner Klose, *Generation im Gleichschritt* (Oldenburg and Hamburg, 1964), pp. 69-72 and 282.
13. Denkschrift (by Schirach) über die Reichsjugend, *BDR*, roll 1.
14. Manfred Priepke, *Die Evangelische Jugend im Dritten Reich, 1933-1936* (Hanover and Frankfurt, 1960), p. 124.
15. *NA*, roll 193, frames 2732102-08.
16. *Ibid.*
17. *Kath. Jung.*, p. 223, fn. 71.
18. *Ibid.*, pp. 111-12.
19. Anordnung Nr. 183/35 vom 24.8.1935, *BRD*, roll 1.
20. *Kath. Jung., Regs.* 98 and 99, pp. 125-28.
21. Helmreich, *Religious Education*, p. 162.
22. *Kirche und NS*, pp. 360-361; *Kath. Jung., Reg.* 105, pp. 54 and 120; p. 222, fn. 61.
23. *Kath. Jung., Reg.* 106, p. 109.
24. *Kirchenkampf*, p. 71.
25. Lewy, *The Catholic Church and Nazi Germany*, pp. 128-129.
26. *Kath. Jung.*, pp. 151-52; 131-32.
27. *Ibid.*, pp. 54 and 135-43.

28. *Ibid., Regs.* 147 and 161. In the period from January to June 1938, the circulation of *Die Wacht* increased from 128,000 to 137,000 and the circulation of *Am Scheideweg* nearly doubled, increasing from 73,000 to 134,000. *Kath. Jung.*, p. 197.

Chapter Eleven

1. Friedricks to Ley, Munich, April 23, 1936, Enclosures, Denkschrift über die Reichsjugend, and Entwurf eines Gesetzes über die Führung der Deutschen Jugend (Reichsjugend), *BDR*, roll 1.

2. Ley to Hess, May 11, 1936, *ibid.*

3. Arno Klönne, *Hitlerjugend; die Jugend und ihre Organisation im Dritten Reich* (Hanover and Frankfurt, 1960), p. 20.

4. *Kath. Jung., Reg.* 123, pp. 201-203.

5. *Ibid.*, pp. 209-12.

6. *Ibid., Reg.* 137, pp. 204-207.

7. *Ibid., Reg.* 139, pp. 182-85.

8. *Ibid.*, p. 121.

9. Mary Alice Gallin, *German Resistance to Hitler; Ethical and Factors* (Washington, D. C., Catholic Univ. Press, 1962), pp. 217-18.

10. For Heinrich Roth's notes on the conferences, see *Kath. Jung., Regs.* 183 and 184, pp. 188-95.

11. An investigation of the books of the *Jugendhaus Düsseldorf, e.V.* had begun in December, 1935 and was still under way in July, 1936 when the *Verein* learned that it would likely lose its tax exemptions. The investigation was still under way in November, 1937 when this conference was held.

Conclusion

1. Ernst-Wolfgang Böckenförde, "German Catholicism in 1933," *Cross Currents*, Vol. XI, no. 3 (Summer, 1961), pp. 284 and 297.

2. *Kath. Jung.*, p. 156.

3. Dirks, "Anfänge und Folgen katholischer Jugendbewegung," in *Die Jugendbewegung*, pp. 248-49.

Three interweaving themes form the substance of this book. The first is the course of the autonomous youth movement, which has been the subject of a good study in English by Walter Laqueur: *Young Germany; A History of the German Youth Movement* (London, 1962). A second theme is the conflict between Catholic Church and Nazi totalitarianism, here focused on the conflict over youth. There is now an excellent and balanced study of the broad church-state conflict, John Conway: *The Nazi Persecution of the Churches 1933-45* (London, 1968). Its bibliography can be supplemented with the fine, but neglected study of Ernst Christian Helmreich: *Religious Education in German Schools* (Cambridge, Mass., 1959) and by that of Ludwig Volk's *Der Bayerische Episkopat und der National Sozialismus 1930-1934* (Mainz, 1966).

A third theme is the Hitler Youth and its development. There are two studies in German, Arno Klonne: *Hitlerjugend; die Jugend und ihre Organisation im Dritten Reich* (Hanover and Frankfurt, 1960 and Werner Klose: *Generation im Gleichschritt* (Oldenburg, 1964), but at present there is no study of the subject in English.

Received too late for inclusion in this study are Hans C. Brandenburg: *Die Geschichte der HJ; Wege und Irrwege einer Generation* (Cologne, 1968) and Franz Henrich: *Die Bünde Katholischer Jugendbewegung; Ihre Bedeutung für die liturgische und eucharistische Erneuerung* (Munich, 1968).

INDEX

191